Lessons from Saint Thérèse:

The Wisdom of God's Little Flower

Lessons from Saint Thérèse:

The Wisdom of God's Little Flower

By

John Paul Thomas

My Catholic Life! Inc.

www.mycatholic.life

ISBN-13: 978-1977735836

Excerpts of *The Story of a Soul (L'Histoire d'une Âme): The Autobiography of Saint Thérèse of Lisieux*, London: Burns, Oates & Washbourne, 1912; 8th ed., 1922, edited by Rev. T.N. Taylor. Permission to use under the terms of the Project Gutenberg License: www.gutenberg.net

Special thanks to Gwen and Sue for their many hours of editing and suggestions!

DEDICATION

To our Blessed Mother who was very dear to Saint Thérèse, especially under the title of "Our Lady of the Smile." May the sweet smile of charity which flows from our Mother in Heaven shine on all who read this book and are touched by the faith, hope and charity shining forth from the heart of Saint Thérèse.

BY

JOHN PAUL THOMAS

"John Paul Thomas" is a pen name chosen by this priest in honor of the Apostles Saints John and Thomas and the great evangelist Saint Paul. This name also evokes the memory of the great Pope Saint John Paul II.

John is the beloved Apostle who sought out a deeply personal and intimate relationship with his Savior. Hopefully the writings in this book point us all to a deeply personal and intimate relationship with our God. May John be a model of this intimacy and love.

Thomas is also a beloved Apostle and close friend of Jesus but is best known for his lack of faith in Jesus' resurrection. Though he ultimately entered into a profound faith crying out, "my Lord and my God," he is given to us as a model of our own weakness of faith. Thomas should inspire us to always return to faith after struggling with doubt. For coming he doubted, doubting he saw, seeing he touched, touching he believed, and believing he shared.

As a Pharisee, Paul severely persecuted the early Christian Church. However, after experiencing a powerful conversion, he went on to become the great evangelist to the gentiles, founding many new communities of believers and writing numerous letters found in Sacred Scripture. His writings are deeply personal and reveal a shepherd's heart. He is a model for all as we seek to embrace our calling to spread the Gospel.

A NOTE FROM THE AUTHOR

I have always admired Saint Thérèse and have read her writings on and off over the years. However, I must admit that I never fully understood what it was that made her so great, and why she, above so many others, would be considered a Doctor of the Church. Because she was given this title in 1997 by arguably the greatest pope in modern history, Saint John Paul the Great, I was drawn to inquire more deeply into her life and virtue. What I discovered is that which has been discovered by so many others since the first publication of her autobiography in 1898: the *Story of a Soul* is truly a spiritual masterpiece!

The first manuscript of her autobiography included her memories from childhood through the time she made her final vows as a Carmelite sister. Interestingly, this manuscript shared more than just her memories. It also presented, in vivid detail, the workings of grace on a pure and humble soul. Little Thérèse is seen as a very ordinary child who was blessed with a loving family and who, in turn, loved her family with deep affection and charity. Her autobiography invites the reader to watch how God takes a little child of four and slowly, lovingly, tenderly, firmly and continuously forms her into a saint. It also shows the development of Thérèse's faith as she experienced God call her, correct her, guide her, inspire her and lead her down the path He had chosen for her. Thérèse responded beautifully to that call and devoted her whole being to the complete embrace of God's will for her life.

The last two manuscripts of Sister Thérèse's autobiography are reflected upon in Chapters Nine and Ten of this book. As I prayerfully pondered those two manuscripts, which speak of her Little Way and her life as a religious sister, I was struck by the depth, beauty, wisdom and love that flow from those pages. Her understanding of God and the precepts of His love will help you cut through the complexities of life and redirect your heart to that which is important: God and His perfect law of Love.

Upon completing this book, *Lessons from Saint Thérèse: The Wisdom of God's Little Flower,* I offer one personal conclusion which has already been discovered by countless others over the past century: Saint Thérèse is a beautiful soul! Her heart is pure, free, expressive, gentle, unwavering, perceptive, and imbued with overflowing charity. Her faith was unshakable no matter what suffering she endured. In fact, the deeper her interior and exterior suffering, the more purified and strengthened her faith became. Her hope was a pillar of iron which was immovably directed toward Heaven. Nothing deterred her from her goal and, by God's abundant mercy, she was granted her desire early in life.

The Life of Saint Thérèse is not just for scholars, saints, priests, theologians or consecrated religious. Her life is also for the most ordinary soul to contemplate. Her daily experiences as a child will inspire you and challenge you. Her life as a religious sister will draw you into a deeper reflection upon your own life, offering practical advice for holiness. And her saintly death should help to clarify your own goals in life so that you can more easily direct all your actions to the one and most important goal any one of us could have: Heaven.

Saint Thérèse, you promised that you would not rest in Heaven until the end of the world. Pray for me and win for me an abundance of grace as I ponder the many lessons of your life in these pages. I open myself to the mysteries of Grace and Heaven, and I ask our dear Lord to challenge me, correct me and inspire me in the ways I need most. May your life, dear Little Flower, bloom in my own heart and may the fragrance of God's mercy permeate my soul so that I, like you, may "sing of the mercies of the Lord forever!" Saint Thérèse, pray for us!

CONTENTS

INTRODUCTION

For more than a century, Saint Thérèse of Lisieux, also known as "The Little Flower," has captivated countless minds and hearts. Her simple and pure heart burned with a deep love for our Lord, and that love overflowed into the lives of many. She daily inspired those who knew her, and she continues to inspire those who read her story.

Marie Françoise-Thérèse Martin was born on January 2, 1873 in Rue Saint-Blaise, Alençon, France to Marie-Azélie Guérin (Zélie), and Louis Martin, a jeweler and watchmaker. Her mother, who often called Thérèse her "little angel," died from breast cancer only a few months before Thérèse's fifth birthday. But those early years with her mother had such an impact upon Thérèse that, in many ways, her mother remained with her, in her heart and mind, throughout her life. The love that mother and daughter shared was eternal.

Her father, Louis Martin, who called Thérèse his "little queen," daily manifested his profound love for her, and she looked up to him as her "king." As a child, Thérèse would spend hours with her father as he worked in the garden, desiring to be near him as often as she could. She would regularly accompany him on daily walks that always included a visit to the Blessed Sacrament at the nearby convent in Lisieux. She loved being in his presence and found the satisfaction of the love of God in his fatherly embrace. At age sixty-six, Louis suffered from two strokes, resulting in paralysis. He spent the next three years in a hospital and the final two years of his life at home in the care of his family. His daughters Céline and Léonie were his primary caregivers at home until June 24, 1893, when Léonie entered the Visitation Convent in Caen at a second attempt at religious life. The last year of his life, Céline faithfully cared for their father with the help of their uncle, a maid and a male assistant until his death on July 29, 1894.

Thérèse had four living sisters and four siblings who died at an early age (three died as infants and Hélène at age five). Her living sisters all entered religious life, three of them entering the same Carmelite convent in Lisieux as Thérèse. Her living sisters were:

- Marie, who became a Carmelite in Lisieux, taking the name Sister Marie of the Sacred Heart.
- Pauline, who became Mother Agnes of Jesus in the Lisieux Carmel.
- Léonie, who became Sister Françoise-Thérèse, Visitandine at Caen. Her life of saintly virtue is currently under study for the purpose of possible future canonization.
- Céline, who also became a Carmelite in Lisieux, taking the name Sister Geneviève of the Holy Face.

The relationship that Thérèse had with her sisters was both typical and unique. The girls played together and sometimes fought with one another. Yet, the depth of their love and affection for one another transfigured what was otherwise a normal sibling relationship. Thérèse adored her sisters and loved being with them, and this love was reciprocal.

Thérèse's entire family shared tender, affectionate, and unwavering love for one another. Their home was a true "school of love" and the lessons of love were learned and lived in their home each and every day. In many ways, Thérèse learned about the love of God first and foremost through the love she experienced within her family.

Just before her fifteenth birthday, after overcoming many obstacles, Thérèse received permission from the Bishop of Bayeux to be received into the Carmelite convent. She formally entered as a postulant on April 9, 1888, at the age of fifteen. She embraced religious life and lived it with fervor and devotion, making her temporary vows on January 10, 1889 and her final vows on September 24, 1890. For the next seven years, Sister Thérèse lived the hidden and holy life of a Carmelite nun.

Sister Thérèse began to write her autobiography when she was twenty-one years old, just three years before she was to die, under obedience to her sister Pauline who had recently been elected as Mother Superior, Mother Agnes of Jesus. This autobiography, *The Story of a Soul*, captures the beauty and profundity of her family life, offers beautiful insights into her vocation as a Carmelite nun, and reveals how devoted she was to Jesus, longing to be with Him forever in Heaven, even from the earliest moments of her childhood.

The first manuscript that makes up the *Story of a Soul* includes Sister Thérèse's childhood memories as well as her first years as a religious sister. At age twenty-three, Sister Thérèse contracted tuberculosis and spent more than a year suffering greatly. It was during this time that Sister Thérèse added two more manuscripts to her autobiography. One was written for her sister Marie, Sister Marie of the Sacred Heart, who desired to hear more about Sister Thérèse's spirituality (covered in Chapter 10 of this book). The final manuscript detailed her life as a religious sister and was written under obedience to Mother Marie de Gonzague at the request of Sister Agnes of Jesus (covered in Chapter 9 of this book). This final manuscript was written during the last year of her life after it was discovered she had contracted tuberculosis. She never finished this manuscript as a result of her diminishing health, but her sister, Sister Agnes of Jesus, kept a detailed notebook of Sister Thérèse's last months, which has been printed in a separate book called *Her Last Conversations*. Also available in print are the *Letters of Sister Thérèse of Lisieux*, much of which was first published under the title of *General Correspondence*. Lastly, Sister Thérèse was an avid writer of poetry, prayers and plays, many of which are published in various formats.

Sister Thérèse died on September 30, 1897 surrounded by three of the Martin sisters as well as all of her religious sisters in the Carmelite convent of Lisieux. Her final words were, "Oh!... I love Him!... My God, I...love...Thee!"

A Family of Saints

As mentioned, Thérèse's mother, Zélie, died when Thérèse was only four years old. Her father, Louis, died when Sister Thérèse was twenty-one years old, just three years before Sister Thérèse's own death. Pope Francis canonized both Louis and his wife Zélie, making them the first husband and wife to be canonized together and the first canonized mother and father of an already canonized child.

In 1893, Saint Thérèse's sister Léonie entered the Monastery of the Visitation at Caen and took the name Sister Françoise-Thérèse. She was the only sister of the five who did not become a Carmelite in Lisieux. Sister Françoise-Thérèse died in 1941, and on January 24, 2015 a diocesan inquiry into her possible sanctity was opened. As a result, she is now referred to as "The Servant of God, Léonie Martin." One day, she may, like her sister and parents, receive the glorious titles of "Blessed" and of "Saint."

Though the cause of beatification for each of Saint Thérèse's other sisters has not been opened, there is little doubt that these sisters were true servants of God who were filled with deep holiness. They were a saintly family. Sister Marie of the Sacred Heart died in 1905 of tuberculosis. Mother Agnes of Jesus (Pauline) died on July 28, 1951, and the final Martin sister, Sister Geneviève of the Holy Face (Céline), died February 25, 1959.

Scope of this Book

This book offers 99 short lessons, reflections and prayers from the life of Saint Thérèse. The lessons are based upon Thérèse's own words as she shared her faith and her heart in the pages of the three manuscripts of her autobiography: *Story of a Soul.* Each subsequent reflection attempts to capture one of her countless virtues so as to savor the "fragrance" of this precious little flower of God and to apply it to the reader's daily life. The prayer to conclude each lesson is not written only to be read, it is written to be prayed. You may find it helpful to pray that prayer slowly and meditatively at the end of each lesson and perhaps even return to that prayer at the end of each day, returning especially to the prayers that are most pertinent to your life.

It may be beneficial to use this book as a daily reflection book, reading one lesson each day. Doing so will allow you to ponder one lesson from her saintly life at a time, so as to absorb the sweetness of her love and the depth of her life. However, you might find it just as beneficial to read several lessons at a time.

Additionally, this book is not intended to be a "onetime read." Rather, the lessons we learn from Saint Thérèse's life are worth absorbing throughout life. Therefore, the reflection and prayer after each lesson make this book a helpful source of daily self-examination and prayer throughout life. For those who especially feel inspired by the life of Saint Thérèse, this book will be helpful to return to over and over. You who are parents might also find the lessons of St. Thérèse of benefit in the formation of your children. Telling Little Thérèse's stories will inspire and challenge your children as they grow and mature in their own life of faith.

Chapter One

Earliest Memories

Lesson One — The Story of a Precious Little Soul

Lesson: Saint Thérèse is one of the most beloved saints of our time. Her humble and pure soul is both attractive and inspiring. The heart of Saint Thérèse comes alive for us in her autobiography which begins with these words:

"It is to you, dear Mother, that I am about to confide the story of my soul. When you asked me to write it, I feared the task might unsettle me, but since then Our Lord has deigned to make me understand that by simple obedience I shall please Him best."

To understand Saint Thérèse and to fully appreciate her humility, holiness and wisdom, it is important to understand how her autobiography came about. Saint Thérèse, at that time Sister Thérèse of the Child Jesus, began to write her story when she was twenty-one years of age, just three years before she would go home to Heaven. She began to write out of obedience to Mother Agnes of Jesus, the Superior of their Carmelite convent in Lisieux.

Mother Agnes was actually Thérèse's older sister Pauline, who had been elected Mother Superior in 1893 and served in that role for three years. Sister Marie, the oldest sister to Sister Thérèse and Mother Agnes, was also in the Carmelite Convent of Lisieux. One day in January, 1895, the three sisters were enjoying recreation time together as Sister Thérèse was sharing some of her childhood memories. Mother Agnes recounts the moment this way:

"One evening in the beginning of the year 1895, I was with my two sisters Marie and Thérèse. Sister Thérèse of the Child Jesus told me several happenings of her childhood and Sister Marie of the Sacred Heart (my eldest sister Marie) said to me: 'O Mother, what a pity that all this should not be written down for us. If you were to ask Sister

Thérèse to write down her childhood memories, how much pleasure this would give us!' ...I turned to Sister Thérèse, who laughed as though we were teasing her, and said: 'I order you to write down your memories of your childhood'" (Affidavit by the Reverend Mother Agnes of Jesus. Bayeux Archives, Vol 1).

This background helps to illustrate that the wisdom contained in *The Story of a Soul* is not a scholarly work produced from many years of study, nor is it a carefully worded autobiography written for the whole world to read. Rather, it is an intimate and personal sharing of one simple soul with her most beloved sister.

Thérèse and Pauline had a holy bond that exceeded even the ordinary relationship sisters often share. This bond was deepened with the loss of their mother when Pauline was fifteen years old and Thérèse was only four. Soon after that painful loss, Thérèse declared that her sister Pauline would now be her "new mother." For the next several years, Thérèse and Pauline were very close and shared a beautiful sisterly love. Pauline also showered Thérèse with a mother's love. The two sisters were inseparable, and Thérèse regularly bared her soul to her new mother Pauline.

Fifteen years after the death of their mother, Thérèse received Pauline as her spiritual mother in a new way when Pauline became Mother Agnes in the Carmelite Convent. It was, therefore, to her dear sister and second mother that she began to write the story of her soul and thus began to entrust this beautiful story to the whole world.

Reflection: Oftentimes in life we present ourselves in an exaggerated and misleading way. This tendency is a result of our fear of being judged by another. But imagine if you could share the story of your soul with someone else in a completely carefree way! How would your story read?

Thérèse wrote in a carefree, trusting, open, and honest manner. She never expected that her memoirs would be read far and wide and declared one of the greatest spiritual gifts to the Church of all time. Rather, she wrote her story for one who knew her and loved her unconditionally.

The story behind the *Story of a Soul* is important because it teaches us about trust and honesty. It illustrates the intimacy that we are called to live with others, as well as the fruit of that unconditional love.

Do you have someone in your life with whom you can entrust the intimacy of your soul? Whom do you trust enough to do the same? Seek to build relationships of love that are so deep that you can confidently share the content of your soul.

Dearest Saint Thérèse, you were privileged to bare the depths of your soul with your dear sister and mother in an intimate and open way. You loved her and were loved by her; you trusted her and were trusted by her. Pray for me, that I may express my unconditional love to others so clearly and unwaveringly that I will become a confidant and friend as God desires. Pray that I will have a heart that is honest and trustworthy, one that is caring and compassionate, and one that is merciful and faithful. Saint Thérèse, pray for us.

Lesson Two — Thérèse, the "Field Flower"

Lesson: There are many types of flowers: lilies, roses, daisies. Each one contains its own beauty and fragrance. Some bloom yearlong, others only in the spring, while others bud forth in the heart of the summer's heat. In pondering the lessons of nature, Sister Thérèse stated the following:

> I understood that every flower created by [God] is beautiful, that the brilliance of the rose and the whiteness of the lily do not lessen the perfume of the violet or the sweet simplicity of the daisy. I understood that if all the lowly flowers wished to be roses, nature would lose its springtide beauty, and the fields would no longer be enamelled with lovely hues.

Thérèse also understood "that God's Love is made manifest as well in a simple soul which does not resist His grace as in one more highly endowed." Not everyone could be a rose; otherwise, the diversity of souls would be lost and the unique beauty of each would not stand out, manifesting the beauty of God in its own unique way.

Some souls are like "field flowers." These lowly and simple flowers reveal a particular charism in that God shows His infinite greatness by stooping down from Heaven to bestow His grace upon them. It is through these simple and humble souls that God's profound love is made most evident.

Most people are created by God to be simple and hidden among the masses. But God sees the beauty of every soul He creates, even if the world fails to perceive it. Each "flower" is radiant to Him, and He chooses to descend to each soul He has created so as to manifest His glory through them.

Reflection: At times we all feel as if we are unimportant. We lose focus on the uniqueness of our own lives and fail to see our own inner beauty that was placed there by God Himself.

Know that God has descended to you and desires to bring forth the beauty of your soul. Know that you delight Him and He sees you, loves you, and accepts you as His little child. Your soul becomes truly beautiful the more fully you embrace His perfect will, in small and great ways.

Accept who you are and become who you were made to be by allowing yourself to become conformed to His perfect will. In doing this, you will shine forth as the beautiful "flower" you were made to be.

Dear Little Flower, Saint Thérèse, I thank you for your simplicity and humility. Thank you for the example you set forth when you allowed the great Almighty God to descend into your soul and shine forth in radiant beauty for all to see. Pray for me, that I may also open my soul to the glory of God and allow Him to live within me, shining forth for all to see. Saint Thérèse, pray for us.

Lesson Three — A Flower After the Storm

Lesson: Thérèse shared with her sister that her "soul has been refined in the crucible of interior and exterior trials." Thérèse did not simply say that she has suffered greatly in her life. Rather, she immediately links both her interior and exterior suffering of the past to the *refinement* of her soul. Thérèse saw suffering through the lens of God's purifying grace. She discovered in her suffering the gift of transformation and holiness.

Thérèse suffered in various ways throughout her short life. She suffered greatly at the death of her beloved mother when she was only four years old. Again, she experienced the pain of loss at age nine when her older sister and "new mother" Pauline entered the Carmelite convent. In school, Thérèse suffered what many children undergo when she was teased and mistreated by her classmates for being different. She was naturally very sensitive and scrupulous and this caused her much interior anguish. She also suffered physical illness as a child, as well as in the last year of her life.

Especially as a young nun, Thérèse suffered great darkness in her soul, which is a common experience for those who draw exceedingly close to God. This "darkness" is best described as a loss of all interior consolation and a sense that God is absent. But this darkness was a gift given to her by God to strengthen her faith and to enable her to choose the will of God for the sake of love alone and not for the reward of consolation.

At age twenty-one, Thérèse described herself as "a flower after the storm." She went on to share that all she suffered enabled her to blossom and radiate the love of God. And throughout every "storm" she endured, the Good Shepherd was with her, walking by her side, leading her to the depths of His divine love.

Reflection: What is it that you suffer? Perhaps the loss of a loved one or a broken relationship is the cause of much anguish in your life. Perhaps you are misunderstood by another, misjudged, ridiculed, or mistreated. Perhaps you suffer from depression, loneliness, or another form of interior darkness.

If any of the above describes you, know that, just like Thérèse, God wants to strengthen you through your trials. This is a difficult lesson to understand and even more difficult to accept. But God is all-powerful and is able to use every storm in life to bring nourishment and strength to your soul.

When you experience the hardships of life, turn your eyes to "the flower after the storm." Allow yourself to understand how God can use your suffering to strengthen you and know that He never leaves you during your trials. He is the Good Shepherd and walks through every dark valley you tread. Make an act of faith and love in the midst of your darkness and look forward, with hope, to the day that the sun will shine upon the flower God is nourishing within you.

Dear Saint Thérèse, God's Little Flower, you beautifully weathered the storms of life. Pray for me, that I may be filled with divine hope and that I may imitate your great faith and love so that I, too, will be "refined in the crucible of interior and exterior trials." May your prayers and witness help to mold me into the splendid flower God desires me to become. Saint Thérèse, pray for us.

Lesson Four — Humility and False Humility

Lesson: Many of the great saints have written about the importance of humility, calling it the "mother of all virtues." Humility is best defined as knowing and believing the truth. More specifically, it's knowing the truth about ourselves.

Oftentimes, those who are proud exaggerate their actions and seek to magnify the appearance of their virtue. But sometimes pride can manifest itself in the form of a false humility that keeps us from seeing all the good that God has done in our lives.

> If a little flower could speak, it seems to me that it would tell us quite simply all that God has done for it, without hiding any of its gifts. It would not, under the pretext of humility, say that it was not pretty, or that it had not a sweet scent, that the sun had withered its petals, or the storm bruised its stem, if it knew that such were not the case.

Thérèse perceived the beauty of her soul, knowing that she was beautiful because of God's abundant mercies and not on account of her own merit. She stated that the numerous blessings God had bestowed upon her were "wholly undeserved" and that "she had nothing in herself worthy of attracting Him." Yet, nonetheless, God "showered blessings on her."

True humility does not lead us to hide the truth of the goodness and glory of God alive within us. Rather, it rejoices in the abundant blessings we have received, proclaims those blessings in gratitude to God and gives God the glory for all that He has done. True humility enables us to see not only our sin, but also our virtue as we recognize the one source of all virtue: our merciful God.

Reflection: When you look at your soul, what do you see? Do you struggle with a poor self-image? Or do you carry an inflated and false image of yourself? The only image you should see is that which God sees.

When God looks at your soul, what does He see? Certainly He sees your sin. But if you are willing to look at your sin with honesty and contrition, then your contrition will overshadow your sin in the eyes of God. He will look past your sin so as to gaze upon the many virtues He has planted within you. Perhaps you too will learn to look beyond your sin and see your virtues as God sees them, rejoicing in their beauty and giving glory to God for His abundant mercy in your life.

Dearest Saint Thérèse, you were showered with an abundance of virtue on account of the abundance of your humility and love. God transformed your inner heart into a place of true beauty and manifested His glory for your eyes to see and for you to share with a world in need. Pray for me, that I may imitate your humility and seek to see not only my sin, but also the hand of God at work within me, making me into an image of Himself. Saint Thérèse, pray for us.

Lesson Five — Fixing Your Eyes on Heaven

> Baby is the dearest little rogue; she comes to kiss me, and at the same time wishes me to die. "Oh, how I wish you would die, dear Mamma," she said, and when she was scolded she was quite astonished, and answered: "But I want you to go to Heaven, and you say we must die to go there"; and in her outburst of affection for her Father she wishes him to die too.

Lesson: The above passage comes from a letter written by Thérèse's mother and sent to Pauline, Thérèse's older sister, when Thérèse was around three years old. At this early age, Thérèse had a deep affection for her mother and her father. She was with them constantly and never wanted to be parted from them. But her affection for them was not selfish. Young Thérèse with piercing wisdom, realized that Heaven was what her mother and father were made for and where they would find perfect joy. Therefore, this faith-filled child desired that her parents would die so as to obtain the glories of Heaven.

Thérèse shows us that true love always seeks the good of the other. Though she deeply desired to be in the presence of her parents, she desired their happiness more than her own. This is love in a selfless form and is beautiful and profound wisdom from a little child.

Reflection: Whom do you love with such an unconditional love that you want that person's happiness above your own? Is your love of others often based on selfish motives, or are you able to turn your eyes to the good of those whom you love and make their holiness and happiness the sole desire of your love for them?

Additionally, on a personal level, do you see Heaven as the greatest good in life and the goal of everything you do? When we can look beyond the temporary nature of this world and peer into the realm of eternity, our perspective here on Earth will be changed. We will no longer live for the moment, seek passing satisfactions, or act in selfish ways. When Heaven is our focus, the present moment and all the daily decisions we make will take on new meaning and clarity.

Make Heaven your one and only goal for you and for those whom God has placed in your life. Allow this eternal perspective to become the basis of all you desire and of all your decisions in life.

Dearest Saint Thérèse, you longed for Heaven for yourself and for your parents with a burning desire. Pray for me, that I may also embrace this eternal longing. May your witness inspire me to set all passing joys aside for the one eternal joy that awaits us all. Saint Thérèse, pray for us.

Lesson Six — Profound Confidence in Our Mother

Lesson: One day, Thérèse asked her mother if she, Thérèse, would go to Heaven. Her mother replied, "Yes, if you are good." Thérèse was pleased to hear this but also immediately realized that if she were not good she would go to Hell. However, this possibility did not shake her childlike confidence. She immediately decided what she would do if she were sent to Hell. She told her mother, "I shall fly to you in Heaven, and you will hold me tight in your arms, and how could God take me away then?" Her simple logic was based on her confidence in both the love of her mother and the mercy of God.

Thérèse knew she could cling to her mother, no matter what, because she had always experienced unconditional love and acceptance from her mother. She also knew that her mother would be in the presence of God, no matter what, because she knew her mother had a profound goodness within her soul and a deep closeness to God. Thérèse's confidence in God was also a confidence in the love she gave to and received from her dear mother.

Reflection: Many people struggle with confidence. This is often on account of their fear of what others think of them and because of the fact that they have never experienced the unconditional love of another. If that is you, ponder the love that Thérèse received from her mother. Make her experience a lesson by which you allow your own confidence in God to grow. The truth is that God loves you just as much as He loved little Thérèse. And if Thérèse could have the utmost confidence in the mercy of God by entrusting herself to her mother's arms, then so must you seek to have the same confidence.

Turn today to the loving arms of our Blessed Mother. Her love for you is, indeed, perfect in every way. Just as Thérèse was confident that God would shower mercy upon her if she clung to her earthly mother, you can have confidence in that same mercy if you cling to your Heavenly Mother. Run to her in faith and seek to develop the deepest of confidence in her maternal care. This confidence will enable our Blessed Mother to hold you tightly and present you to God as her precious child.

Dearest Saint Thérèse, you had confidence in the mercy of God because you experienced that profound gift in your relationship with your earthly mother. Pray for me that I may have that same confidence in the motherly care and intercession of our Heavenly Mother. Dearest Mother Mary, receive me into your maternal arms and present me to your Divine Son, Jesus. Saint Thérèse, pray for us.

Lesson Seven — Trusting in Forgiveness

Lesson: One humble quality of Saint Thérèse was that she was not afraid to admit her sin. She knew she failed to love in a perfect way, and she was regularly aware of her weakness. Too often in life, when we fall short of God's glory, we tend to justify our actions and deny our sin. We become self-righteous and obstinate in admitting our guilt.

Thérèse was different. She never hid her sin or weakness. Her mother identified this quality when she said of her little saint, "The moment she has done anything mischievous, everyone must know." Whether she fought with her sister, was negligent in some duty, or acted in a way that was rude,

Thérèse not only immediately felt sorrow for her sin, she also admitted it openly and apologized profusely.

One reason Thérèse was so willing to admit her sin was that she trusted in forgiveness. She experienced a profound level of forgiveness from her family and, through them, discovered the forgiveness of God. By having full confidence in the gift and transforming power of forgiveness and reconciliation, Thérèse regularly ran to this gift, fully expecting to receive it from whomever she asked.

Reflection: How do you approach sin in your life? You are a sinner, that is a fact. Are you able to admit this with honesty and ease? If it is difficult to admit that you are a sinner, then step back and look at the merciful Heart of our God. It is impossible to see our sin, admit our guilt, and repent of what we have done unless we are aware of the merciful Heart of God.

God does not desire your condemnation or punishment. Instead, He longs for you to be free of the burdens that your sins cause. If you can start with this understanding of forgiveness and God's abundant mercy, fear of confessing your sins openly will be alleviated.

Allow your confidence in God's mercy to grow so that you, like Saint Thérèse, will repent the moment you fall short of God's glory and turn back as soon as you stray from His perfect will. Building a habit of immediate repentance will lighten the heaviest burden you could carry in life.

Dearest Saint Thérèse, I thank you for the holy witness of your sorrowful heart. You did not hesitate to admit your sin and to seek the forgiveness of others. You understood the mercy of God and sought that mercy from those whom you offended. Pray for me, that I may seek the same freedom you experienced by your humble contrition. Saint Thérèse, pray for us.

Lesson Eight — The Power of Human Love

Lesson: Charity must be the central mission of every follower of Christ. Charity is an act of supreme selflessness by which we are called to rely upon grace to put the good of another before ourselves. It's selfless and self-giving.

While charity is a supernatural grace from God, made possible only by the death and resurrection of Jesus, there is another form of love which is also very powerful. This love may be called "natural love." Natural love is greatly helped by grace (charity) but is distinct in that it's more of an affection or attraction to something good. When natural love is experienced in a relationship, then the attraction is to the person who is innately good. When natural love mixes with supernatural charity, one not only fulfills the central Christian mission of laying down one's life for another, but also receives the profound gift of the love and affection of another. This natural love takes place in spousal love but also extends to other family members and friends.

Saint Thérèse experienced this form of natural love to a profound degree within her own family, and especially with her sister Pauline. On many occasions, while Pauline had been away at boarding school, Thérèse's mother would ask her young daughter, "What are you thinking about?" As Thérèse sat quietly pondering in silence, her answer was always the same, "Pauline!" The natural sisterly bond that Thérèse and Pauline shared was the source of much human satisfaction. When Pauline was not around, Thérèse felt her absence. This is natural love and human affection as God designed it to be lived.

Reflection: Do you have human friendships that are the source of much satisfaction and fulfillment in life? Too often, our affection for others becomes distorted and selfish, contrary to the natural design of God. But when supernatural charity is infused into a relationship, and when both persons love with the grace of God, a powerful and holy natural bond is also formed.

Reflect upon the holy friendships you have had in life that have produced an abundance of satisfaction and fulfillment. If these friendships are centered in Christ, then you can be assured that the satisfaction you experience is a result of the natural fruit of God's design of human love.

On the contrary, when a relationship causes much hurt in your life, step back and examine your side of the relationship to be sure that your sin is not depriving you or the other of the natural blessings of your shared love. When love is holy, it is also deeply satisfying. Allow the good fruits of your friendships to guide you into a greater experience of the gift of human love.

Dearest Saint Thérèse, your sisterly affection for Pauline was a true gift from God. The fruit of that holy bond is an inspiration to all who seek to deepen their love for others. Pray for me, and for all families, that the love shared in my life and in every home may always achieve the natural end that was intended by God. May your witness, and that of Pauline's, inspire us and lead us to a deeper love and affection for all whom God places in our lives. Saint Thérèse, pray for us.

Lesson Nine — Mother Knows Best

Lesson: Parents know their children in ways that only they are capable of knowing. In fact, observant and dedicated parents will often know their children better than their children know themselves. Such was the case with Thérèse and her mother.

Thérèse's mother was aware of a certain self-love, as well as a stubborn streak, that Thérèse had as a child. But she was also aware that Thérèse responded contritely when confronted with her shortcomings and quickly changed from self-love to virtue.

On one occasion, wanting to test the limits of her daughter's self-love, her mother said, "Thérèse, if you will kiss the ground, I will give you a halfpenny." A halfpenny was a fortune in those days for a child and was certainly something that any child would desire. But upon receiving such an offer from her mother, Thérèse responded defiantly, "No, thank you, Mamma, I would rather go without it."

The lesson was not lost on Thérèse. She never forgot about this gentle invitation from her mother and eventually realized that her mother was only helping her to see her own need to grow in humility. It takes a caring mother to teach such a subtle lesson to her daughter. But Thérèse was a good learner, and this small challenge to her pride enabled her to see this tendency toward pride and overcome it quickly.

Reflection: When someone challenges your pride, offers a gentle correction, or highlights your sinful tendencies, how do you respond? It's so very easy to initially respond like Thérèse did, with defiance. But even if you do find that initial tendency within you, seek to imitate Thérèse by letting the lessons others teach you to sink in.

When the words of another bothers you in some way, do not react with anger, self-will, stubbornness or pride. Rather, allow that person's words to be the source of your own examination of conscience. Even if a comment or correction is very slight, be attentive to any initial negative reaction on your part. Very often, what bothers you the most is more on account of your own sin than it is on account of the judgmentalness or rudeness of another. In fact, what you perceive as another's sin might not be sin at all. It might be love, given to you in the form of correction and guidance. Don't miss out on these subtle, or even not so subtle, acts of love God gives you so can grow in virtue.

Dearest Saint Thérèse, you were greatly blessed by a mother who loved you dearly. She loved you with such a powerful love that she was willing to offer you even the smallest correction when you needed it.

Pray for me, that I may receive all correction with love and humility. May I imitate your willingness to listen and change when I am invited to do so by the love and care of others. Saint Thérèse, pray for us.

Lesson Ten — Small Sacrifices

Lesson: Thérèse was aware of the power of making small daily sacrifices. In 1876, when Thérèse was only three, her mother wrote, "Even Thérèse is anxious to make sacrifices. Marie has given her little sisters a string of beads on which to count their acts of self-denial." Her mother spoke about how she delighted in hearing her daughters speak about spiritual matters but then went on to emphasize, "But it is more amusing still to see Thérèse put her hand in her pocket, time after time, to pull a bead along the string, whenever she makes a little sacrifice."

For a child of three to understand the power of small sacrifices and to intentionally make them time and time again is more than inspiring. This shows how serious Thérèse was about loving God, and it points to her wisdom in that she comprehended the value of sacrifice. It also reveals that she put this wisdom into action by trusting that God would receive every sacrifice she offered Him.

Thérèse's habit came about because her older sister Marie gave her beads to count her sacrifices. Once again, we see that Thérèse was easily formed in the ways of God and responded to the loving guidance given to her by her family. She lived in a school of faith and love.

Reflection: How aware are you of the power of small sacrifices? It could be said that small acts of love are not just important, they are everything! We are rarely called to make huge sacrifices, requiring heroic acts of love. Opportunities to make small acts of love in the form of small sacrifices occur every day, however.

If you were to count the small sacrifices you make out of love every day, how many beads would you need? Kindness, gentleness, mercy and the like are best expressed in small intentional ways. Others might never see the small sacrifices we make, but those sacrifices make a difference nonetheless. Small sacrifices, done regularly and intentionally, have the ability to form our character. They form us in charity since charity is best defined as "sacrificial love."

Make it your goal to acquire a permanent habit of small sacrifices. A habit can only be formed by doing these sacrifices day after day, week after week, and year after year. The more you offer sacrifice, the more you will want to sacrifice. And the more you want to sacrifice, the more you will become an instrument of sacrificial love.

Dearest Saint Thérèse, you learned from a very young age about the power contained in small sacrifices of love. Pray for me, that I may also be as open as you were to these lessons of love. Help me to form a deep habit of self-giving so that I may become the saint that God is calling me to be. Saint Thérèse, pray for us.

Lesson Eleven — I Choose Everything!

Lesson: One day, Léonie decided she was too old to play with dolls and so she presented a basket full of doll accessories to her sisters Thérèse and Céline. Céline took one item and then, Thérèse, after looking through the basket declared, "I choose everything!" Though this was a small act of selfishness, a lesson was learned by Thérèse. She later shared that this desire for everything became her desire as it pertains to the will of God, and this childish incident became a forecast of her whole life:

> My God, I choose everything, I will not be a Saint by halves, I am not afraid of suffering for Thee, I only fear one thing, and that is to do my own will. Accept the offering of my will, for I choose all that Thou willest.

Thérèse realized that being lukewarm in her faith was not an option if she were to become a saint. If she were to achieve the sanctity that she desired, she would need to allow her own will to disappear so that only the will of God would remain. "Not my will but yours be done" (Luke 22:42).

She also realized that by surrendering fully to the will of God, she would encounter suffering in life. But suffering, when it comes as a result of doing the will of God, is not something that should cause us fear. Rather, suffering must be fully embraced as a consequence of walking in the footsteps of Jesus. Thérèse's desire was to live out the will of God to the greatest extent possible, no matter the cost.

Reflection: Are you willing to choose everything contained within the will of God? Are you willing to let go of your own will, your own ideas and your own preferences so that only God's will can be done in your life?

At first, this sounds like a good idea, and many will respond with a clear, "Yes." But don't answer that question too quickly. Ponder first the "consequences" of choosing everything contained within the will of God. This choice is radical, total, and requires the utmost sacrifice of your life in imitation of Jesus.

What might God ask of you? How hard will it be to say "Yes" to every detail of God's perfect will? Saying "Yes" to God will be painful in that it will have the effect of purifying you of all selfishness and sin. It hurts to be purged, but it's the only way to holiness.

Say "Yes" with Saint Thérèse and continue to choose everything in imitation of her example. Whatever suffering you endure on account of this choice will produce blessings a hundredfold.

My dearest Saint Thérèse, you did not hesitate to say "Yes" to God with all your strength. You chose everything contained within His will and rejected all that was contrary to it. Pray for me, that I may not hesitate in doing the will of God for my life. If I suffer, help me to know that every sacrifice I make will be repaid by God in ways beyond my imagination. Saint Thérèse, pray for us.

Lesson Twelve — Fear Not the Evil One

Lesson: When Thérèse was a child, she had a dream of two hideous little devils dancing on a barrel in the garden. When they saw her, they ran from her and hid. In her dream, she overcame her initial fear and pursued the devils to see what they were doing. When she found them, she discovered that the frightful little devils were actually hiding out of fear of her!

Later in life, Thérèse never forgot about this dream and shared the lesson that she learned from it. She said, "Of course this dream was nothing extraordinary; yet I think Our Lord made use of it to show me that a soul in the state of grace has nothing to fear from the devil, who is a coward, and will even fly from the gaze of a little child."

Thérèse realized that the evil one is real, hideous and vile in every way. However, she also realized that when one's soul is in a state of grace, the evil one cannot inflict harm upon it. Therefore, the devil fears those holy souls who do battle with him by their sanctity of lives.

Reflection: What do you fear in life? The evil one is a master at causing irrational fear in our lives. But the truth that we learn from little Thérèse is that when we live a life of holiness, the evil one is far more fearful of us than we are of him.

This may be a hard lesson for many to learn. Most people do not think of the evil one very often, and that might be good. But take a moment to think about this hideous creature. The evil one hates you with a perfect hate. He desires only your utter destruction and eternal death. If this is disheartening and discouraging to think about, then ponder also the fact that this hideous creature has no power over you unless you allow him to have that power. And the only way you allow him to have power over your life is by sinning.

When you sin, especially when your sin is grave and unrepented, the evil one is able to have his way with you. He will inflict upon you feelings of hate, envy, lust, selfishness and the like. He will distort your passions, confuse your thinking and lead you astray.

On the contrary, when you seek to eliminate all sin from your life, the Holy Spirit alone takes possession of your precious soul. Within your soul, He places mercy, kindness, gentleness, self-control and the like. Therefore, the devil is defeated within a soul who is immersed in the grace of God.

Dearest Saint Thérèse, you did not fear the evil one in your life because your love of God was so deep that the evil one had no power over you. Pray for me that I may turn from all sin in my life and may be freed of the many snares and enticements of the devil. Place in my heart, through your prayers, the many fruits of the Holy Spirit so that I will walk in the presence of God, free of all fear and all sin. Saint Thérèse, pray for us.

Lesson Thirteen — The Starting Point for Virtue

Lesson: Our human nature is the starting point for all virtue. Unfortunately, Original Sin has severely disfigured our human nature, leaving us with physical, mental, emotional and moral defects. The moral defects we experience come from what we call concupiscence, which is the disordered tendency we experience toward sin.

Some people struggle deeply with various natural disorders, while others appear to struggle far less, having what appears to be many natural gifts of intelligence, personality, self-control and the like. God knows the "starting point" that each one of us has and will judge us accordingly to the degree that we allow grace to build upon our nature.

Thérèse was quite gifted on a natural level. Not only does she appear to have been quite intelligent, she also had many good natural qualities upon which grace could build. For example, Thérèse reveals the following natural tendency she had toward the good: "Even if I was unjustly accused, I preferred to keep silence. There was no merit in this, for I did it naturally."

This is a great natural blessing she discovered within herself. Most people rebel strongly if they are unjustly accused and react with much distress, emotion and passion. But Thérèse had such a wholesome nature that she admitted she did not earn any "merit" from her ability to humbly accept unjust accusations. It was simply part of who she was, naturally speaking. Though Thérèse's natural humility was great, she did allow grace to build upon her natural gift so as to bring this virtue to greater perfection. As she did this, she also earned much merit in the eyes of God.

Thérèse also spoke about her "naturally happy disposition" which "helped to make life bright." Again, this natural gift of a happy disposition no doubt made not only her life bright but also had a wonderful effect on others.

Reflection: What are your natural gifts? Perhaps they are different from what Saint Thérèse manifested, but you do have natural gifts that stand out above the rest. Very often, we rely upon our natural gifts and use them for good. But it's also likely that those who have many natural gifts will fail to allow grace to build upon them so as to bring forth even more virtue on a supernatural level.

Instead of looking at your greatest struggles and natural weaknesses, ponder, today, some of your greatest natural gifts. Examine how well you offer those gifts to God and use them for good. Don't squander what you have been blessed with. Allow the goodness you have in your human nature to grow and blossom so that you will merit countless rewards from our merciful God.

Dearest Saint Thérèse, you were blessed with numerous natural gifts from God. Among them was your humility. You did not allow the injustice you experienced in life to deter you from love and to leave you distressed. Pray for me, that I may discover the ways that God has blessed me on a natural level so that I may offer those gifts to God and allow Him to transform them into even greater perfection by His grace. Saint Thérèse, pray for us.

Chapter Two

A Catholic Household

Lesson Fourteen — The Glory of Heaven

Lesson: During the final weeks of their mother's illness, a family friend picked up Thérèse and Céline and cared for them every day. However, even though they were not with their mother, she was always on their minds.

One day when Céline was given an apricot, she leaned over to Thérèse to tell her that she would give it to their mother so her mother could enjoy its sweetness. But Thérèse realized that her mother was now too ill for such a delight. She recounted, "Alas! our beloved Mother was now too ill to eat any earthly fruit; she would never more be satisfied but by the glory of Heaven. There she would drink of the mysterious wine which Jesus, at His Last Supper, promised to share with us in the Kingdom of His Father."

Little Thérèse and Céline had their eyes fixed on their mother, but also on the glory of Heaven! They loved their mother and this love led them to desire Heaven for her. Though her illness and death left them with much sorrow, they were consoled by their knowledge that their mother would soon be with Jesus in Heaven. Recall, also, how Thérèse, as a child of three, said to her mother, "Oh, how I wish you would die, dear Mamma!" (See Lesson Five)

The greatest consolation we can obtain, at the death of a loved one, is our knowledge of what awaits them in Heaven. This knowledge can lift the heavy burden of grief and redirect all feelings of sadness.

Reflection: How completely are you able to put your eyes upon the glories of Heaven? You must long for Heaven for yourself and for all whom you love. However, this may often be quite a challenge to do. It may instead be far easier to turn to the troubles of your daily life and lose sight of your eternal destiny.

Living with your eyes fixed upon Heaven is not a denial of your life here on Earth. Rather, by allowing this eternal perspective to become your daily focus, all that you encounter each day is put into perspective. Each action of your day must be motivated by a longing to be with God forever in Heaven. Heaven must be your singular goal.

Allow yourself, this day, to imitate the faith of little Thérèse and Céline. Allow them to inspire you and to teach you the meaning and purpose of life.

Dearest Saint Thérèse, as your mother lay dying, your heart was filled with sorrow, but it was also filled with joy as she was so very close to Heaven. Pray for me, that I may keep my eyes on the ultimate goal of life and will never fail to do all things so as to achieve the purpose of life. In the end, all that matters is Heaven. May this truth be the lens through which I see every action of my life and the motivation for everything I do. Saint Thérèse, pray for us.

Lesson Fifteen — The Wound of Love

Lesson: When Thérèse lost her mother, she recounted that this loss affected her deeply:

> I must tell you that after my Mother's death my naturally happy disposition completely changed. Instead of being lively and demonstrative as I had been, I became timid, shy, and extremely sensitive; a look was enough to make me burst into tears.

Fortunately, she had the loving care of her father, whose "heart seemed endowed with a mother's love," and was also cared for by her sisters, who "were no less tender and devoted." But despite the great blessing of her father and sisters, she missed her mother terribly.

Loss affects us all in different ways. Thérèse, being quite affectionate, felt her mother's absence deeply. She lost her naturally happy disposition and became shy and timid instead. This experience was not so much a result of her weakness; rather, her profound feelings of loss were a result of how deeply she loved.

It may be surprising to discover that the more ardently we love, the more vulnerable we are to sorrow and hurt. Those who love little will lose little when their loved one is taken away. But those who love much will lose much when their loved one is taken away.

As a result, some will choose to love little so as to avoid the potential for hurt. But doing so would be a tragedy. It is much better to love with all your heart, even if that love ends with much hurt.

The sorrow in Thérèse's heart was a wound of love. She bore that wound well, allowed the balm of her father's and sisters' love to help heal it, and grew stronger in character as a result. A heart that loves, experiences loss, and then heals through love is a heart that is truly blessed.

Reflection: How deeply do you love in life? Some are afraid to love or to let themselves be loved. Others give and receive love in a disordered way. But when love is pure and holy, be it among spouses, children, siblings or friends, the joy experienced from that love is profound.

Are you willing to be vulnerable in life and to take the risk of giving another your heart? Do not hesitate. And, in the end, if your love results in hurt or loss, seek healing, have hope and make the choice to love again.

Dearest Saint Thérèse, as a young child you loved your mother with a pure love. Her death left a deep wound in your heart, but it was a wound of love. As a result, the wound healed in such a way as to make your heart even more capable of love. Pray for me, that I may give my heart completely out of love to others, becoming vulnerable to both the great joys of love and the potential hurts that may result. May I imitate your pure love now and always. Saint Thérèse, pray for us.

Lesson Sixteen — The King and Little Queen of Lisieux

Lesson: After his wife's death, Thérèse's father moved with his daughters from Alençon to Lisieux to live near their mother's brother Isidore Guérin and his wife Céline Fournet and daughters Jeanne and Marie. The girls' aunt took on a motherly role for her nieces. The Martins moved into a new home and their healing continued. Thérèse stated about this period in her life, "I cried and fretted for my Mother; but here my little heart expanded, and I smiled on life once more."

In Lisieux, Thérèse spent many hours with her father. They went on long walks, she played in the garden as her father worked, they enjoyed fishing expeditions and picnics, and she was introduced to the Carmelite nuns for the first time. During this first encounter, her father said to Thérèse, "Look, little Queen, behind that big grating there are holy nuns who are always praying to Almighty God." Nine years later, Thérèse would be among them.

Later in life, as Thérèse recounted the many wonderful experiences she had with her father in Lisieux, she wrote to Pauline, "I should never stop if I told you of the thousand

and one incidents of this kind that I can remember. How shall I make you understand the love that my Father lavished on his little Queen!"

It was the tragedy of her mother's death that brought this "little Queen" to Lisieux. But in God's providence, and through the daily care of her "king," this queen would become the greatest saint Lisieux had ever known.

Reflection: God's ways are not our ways nor are His thoughts ours.   His ways and His thoughts are infinitely above our own (Cf. Isaiah 55:8-9).   Without experiencing the loss of her dear mother, at the age of four, Thérèse and her family would have never moved to Lisieux.   And if they never moved to Lisieux, Thérèse and her sisters would most likely never have entered into the Carmelite convent, which became their new Heaven on Earth.   From the walls of that convent, the world has been taught so many beautiful lessons about love.

What has happened in your life that brought about something unexpected or unplanned?   Too often when the unexpected happens, we have a hard time adjusting and accepting the change.   But change can lead to the fullness of life that God has in store for us.   Sometimes the change we experience in life is painful; sometimes it may not be.   The bottom line is that God uses the ordinary circumstances of our life, however they unfold, to do great things through us.

Thérèse and her family did not anticipate that their move to Lisieux would ultimately result in so many blessings for the Church and world.   Too often, we do not realize that the daily circumstances in which we find ourselves may actually be the beginning of God's glorious will for our lives.

Reflect, today, upon any unexpected situation you find yourself in. Look at it with hope and anticipation of all that God has in store for you. You may not see the good fruits immediately, but if you are faithful to the daily will of God, the end will one day be glorious.

Dearest Saint Thérèse, your move with your family to Lisieux was due to the tragic loss of your mother. But through that tragedy, God did great things in your life and in the lives of your family. Through you all, He brought great blessings upon the Church. Pray for me, that I may accept every change in my life with faith and with love, knowing that God will do great things through me if only I remain faithful to His perfect plan. Saint Thérèse, pray for us.

Lesson Seventeen — The Gentle Almighty

Lesson: While Thérèse was on a picnic with her father, a storm suddenly appeared. Thérèse recounted two images from that storm. First, she said, "A thunderbolt fell in a field close by, and, far from feeling the least bit afraid, I was delighted——it seemed that God was so near." Quickly, her father picked her up and they made their way through the fields to safety. As they did, Thérèse recalled, "In spite of his fishing tackle, he carried me in his arms while I looked down on the beautiful jewelled drops, almost sorry that I could not be drenched by them."

These two images from nature impressed little Thérèse: the "thunderbolt" and the "beautiful jewelled drops." Why was it that these two images from creation impressed her so much?

First, we know that God is the Almighty. His power is perfect in that He can do all things. Most children who witness a thunderbolt would run in fear. But for Thérèse, she saw the closeness of God, the closeness of the Almighty God who contained all power within Himself.

But God is not only the Almighty, He is also our most tender and gentle Father. Thérèse saw these "beautiful jewelled drops" and saw in them a reflection of the drenching love of a most gentle Father in Heaven, seen also in her earthly father who carried her in his arms.

Creation is capable of many lessons. Nature itself reveals the power, splendor, goodness and mercy of God in countless ways. When we have a simple faith, and eyes that are attentive, we will not miss the reflection of God all around us.

Reflection: Do you see the presence of God in creation? First and foremost, you must seek to recognize God reflected in the soul of every person, including your own soul. From there, you must seek to discover the reflection of God in nature and in all that God has made.

Spend time, this week, paying attention to the way God reveals Himself in that which He has made. Ponder your own soul, the souls of others, the gentle breeze, the morning sky and the starry night. Listen to God speak, and allow Him to reveal His many attributes and His love.

Dearest Saint Thérèse, you were attentive to the many ways that God is reflected in all of creation. Pray for me, that I may also encounter the divine presence wherever I go. May I imitate your simple faith and your humble intuitiveness. Saint Thérèse, pray for us.

Lesson Eighteen — Our Response to Rejection

Lesson: As Thérèse and her father would walk through the streets of Lisieux, Thérèse loved to give alms to the poor. One day, she saw a man who was crippled and gave him a penny. He smiled and refused this gift, causing Thérèse much sorrow.

Perhaps he was embarrassed to be offered this alm from a six year old girl, or perhaps he didn't need it. But his refusal did not cause Thérèse to give up on her act of charity. Instead, she remembered that she once heard that God never refuses the prayers that are prayed on the day of your First Communion. At that moment, though her First Communion was still five years away, Thérèse resolved to pray for this man on that day. Sure enough, she never forgot about this promise and on the day of her First Communion, she entrusted this man to God through her prayers.

Reflection: Sometimes our acts of love are rejected by another. As a result, many will choose not to persevere in their charity. Thérèse was different. This refusal only caused her to be more determined in her love and it elevated her gift from a penny to a powerful prayer that

God could not refuse. We also must be determined never to cease offering God's love to others.

Have you attempted to reach out to another in love, only to have that love rejected? This painful experience can lead to discouragement. Rejection is hard to overcome.

Spend time today reflecting upon any experience you have had like this. Reflect, also, upon how you responded to this rejection. Seek to imitate little Thérèse and commit yourself to pray for those who have rejected your love. No one can reject our prayer, and our prayer is often the most important gift we can give.

Dearest Saint Thérèse, you set a beautiful example of perseverance in love when you chose to pray for that crippled man on the day of your First Communion. Pray for me, that I may also imitate your devotion and charity. May I always offer the good alm of prayer for those from whom I have experienced any form of rejection. Saint Thérèse, pray for us.

Lesson Nineteen — Learning From Our Mistakes

Lesson: One evening, in May of 1878, when Thérèse was only five, her sisters left her at home while they attended May devotions at church. They decided Thérèse was too young to attend. However, this did not stop her from her devotions.

She arranged an altar and asked the maid, Victoire, to attend her service. Victoire happily obliged and brought with her two candles, which she knew would delight Thérèse. At first she hid the candles in her apron, wanting Thérèse to light the very small candles she already had, knowing they would go out quickly, so that she could then surprise Thérèse with her gift.

Thérèse did light her two small candles and asked Victoire to pray the *Memorare* as her tiny candles burned. Instead of praying the prayer, Victoire laughed, knowing that once the candles burned she would surprise Thérèse. Thérèse, however, became quite angered at Victoire's laughing and cried out, "Victoire, you naughty girl!" Shocked, Victoire showed Thérèse the new candles she had hidden, and Thérèse realized that Victoire's laugh was on account of her excitement at the gift rather than at Thérèse. Thérèse immediately felt much sorrow at what she had said and quickly learned a powerful lesson about anger. She firmly resolved, after that incident, never to lose her temper like that again.

Reflection: What mistakes have you made in life in which you ignored the lessons you could have learned? Sometimes, when we sin, we justify or rationalize our act and fail to learn and grow. Other times, we act as if our sin was "no big deal," and we end up offering only a muted apology, failing to make a resolute change.

Do not let the lessons your sins can teach you go unlearned. God can use even the smallest sin to help us grow in holiness. Once we repent of our sins, be they big or small, God not only forgives, He also transforms our sin into a source of holiness.

Dearest Saint Thérèse, though you were not perfect, you were quick to acknowledge your sin and you were quick to change. Pray for me, that I may always see my sin clearly. May I humble myself when faced with my sin and, through repentance, grow in virtue and holiness of life. Saint Thérèse, pray for us.

Lesson Twenty — Impressed by Grace

Lesson: Looking back on her First Confession, Thérèse states: "I came out of the Confessional more joyful and lighthearted than I had ever felt before." She was deeply impressed with numerous blessings she discovered within that holy Sacrament.

First, when Pauline told her that she would be confessing her sins directly to God when she confessed to the priest, Thérèse believed her sister and asked her if she could tell Father Ducellier that she loved him with her "whole heart" since it was really God to whom she would be speaking to through him.

After her confession, she asked Father Ducellier to bless her rosary, which he did. On their walk home, Thérèse stopped to gaze at her newly blessed rosary with awe. When Pauline asked her what she was doing, she responded, "I am seeing what a blessed rosary looks like."

Thérèse was able to see the grace of God with her eyes of faith. First, she saw God in the priest when she confessed to him. Second, she realized that her rosary was now changed by a blessing and hoped to discover the change with her own eyes.

Though grace is not immediately visible to the eye, we must seek to perceive its effects, and we must allow ourselves to be deeply impressed by the way God comes to us through countless instruments and in varied ways.

Reflection: Are you impressed by the working of grace all around you? Do you see God's grace at work? God is present to you in the most profound way through the Sacraments, including in the person of your priests. His grace also comes to you through the Holy Scriptures, through sacred images and other blessed objects. He is present in every act of charity you encounter and in numerous other ways.

Reflect upon how attentive you are to the presence of grace all around you. If you do not see this grace, seek to imitate the simple faith of little Thérèse. Allow your eyes to be opened so that you will be in awe of God every time He showers His blessings upon you.

Dearest Saint Thérèse, your simple faith allowed you to see God present to you in the many ways that you encountered Him every day. You discovered Him in the Sacraments, in your blessed rosary, and in many other aspects of your life. You were impressed by grace and in awe of it. Pray for me, that I may also have the eyes of faith necessary to perceive the work of God as He comes to me each and every day. Saint Thérèse, pray for us.

Lesson Twenty-One — A Lesson from the Sunday Feast!

Lesson: Most children dream of exciting events such as festivals, sleepovers, parties and the like. Yet, what caused little Thérèse much excitement were the feasts of the Church year.

> The feasts! What precious memories these simple words bring to me. I loved them; and my sisters knew so well how to explain the mysteries hidden in each one. Those days of earth became days of Heaven.

Above all, she loved to attend the procession of the Blessed Sacrament. Her heart was especially filled with joy when she was able to throw flowers toward the Sacred Monstrance carrying our Lord, so as to express her love for Him. She also had a deep love for the weekly feast of Sunday, the Lord's day, and it brought her much joy to attend the Holy Mass with her family.

She recounts that, even though she would always listen attentively to the sermon at Mass, she would also learn much wisdom simply be watching her father's face.

> I must own I looked at Papa more than at the preacher, for I read many things in his face. Sometimes his eyes were filled with tears which he strove in vain to keep back; and as he listened to the eternal truths he seemed no longer of this earth, his soul was absorbed in the thought of another world

What a beautiful way for this small child to hear the Word of God. She listened to the priest at Sunday Mass but was also attentive to the way the priest's words affected her father. Her father's reception of the Word of God was evident, and little Thérèse was nourished by the Word of God as it radiated from his face.

Reflection: We teach many lessons in life by our words, but we teach just as many by our actions and even by our demeanor. Parents especially share the Word of God with their children by allowing God's Word to illuminate their countenance as their children quietly observe.

Ponder this lesson from two perspectives. First, who radiates the Word of God to you? Be attentive to that person and listen to the "sermon" their holiness of life teaches. Allow the presence of God in their life to teach you, lead you and make you holy.

Secondly, ponder the great importance of engaging in holy Mass each week. First and foremost, this is for the good of your own soul, but your fidelity is also for the eyes of many others. Allow others, especially your family, to see your active life of faith, and do not hide your deep love of God from them. God desires to use you, and even your holy demeanor, to share the great mysteries of His love.

Dearest Saint Thérèse, you were like a sponge, soaking up the Word of God in many ways. You were attentive to sermons and feasts and were also attentive to the faith that radiated from the face of your father. Pray for me, that I may also be attentive to the grace of God radiating from the face of others. As I do, may God shine brightly from my life for all to see. Saint Thérèse, pray for us.

Lesson Twenty-Two — Led by Faith

Lesson: On various occasions, when Thérèse was walking at night with her father, she would look up at the stars and gaze upon them. Upon seeing what appeared to be the letter "T" in Orion's Belt, Thérèse was impressed.

> "Look, Papa," I would cry, "my name is written in Heaven!" Then, not wishing to see this dull earth any longer, I asked him to lead me, and with my head thrown back, I gazed unweariedly at the starry skies.

Though this was a simple act of a child, we can discover much meaning in its symbolism. First, as on other occasions, Thérèse admired the beauty of God's creation. The stars were fascinating to her, no doubt because they were partly a reflection of the transcendence and magnificence of God.

Secondly, Thérèse was able to throw her head back to gaze at the stars as she walked with her father at night, because she trusted her father to guide her steps. Her utter confidence in the care of her father freed her to gaze at the heavens.

This same confidence must be present in our lives as we walk by faith. This world and our journey through it is filled with darkness at times. But through that darkness we are bathed with countless tiny bright lights of grace and mercy. These gifts of grace are as countless as the stars, and we will be aware of them only if we abandon ourselves in trust to the guidance of our Father in Heaven.

Reflection: How freely do you abandon yourself and trust in the guiding hand of God in your life? We are called to walk by faith in this life, not by our own sight. Do you walk by faith?

Ponder this precious image of little Thérèse being guided along the way by her father as she gazed toward the heavens, soaking in the magnificence of God's creation. Let that image teach you to trust in God with a childlike confidence. Do not hesitate or else you will miss the multitude of God's grace.

Dearest Saint Thérèse, you trusted in your father's guiding hand with a childlike confidence. The confidence you had in your father was the same confidence you had in your loving God. Pray for me, that I may completely abandon myself to the Father in Heaven and, being guided by His gentle hand, walk in awe of the countless graces He bestows upon the world. Saint Thérèse, pray for us.

Lesson Twenty-Three — Loving Attentiveness to Weakness

Lesson: Pauline, Thérèse's older sister and "new mother," was very good at caring for Thérèse and helping her mature in character. One motherly quality that Pauline exercised over little Thérèse was her attentiveness to the smallest faults that Thérèse had, so as to help her overcome them. One area of growth Pauline wanted Thérèse to overcome was small fears, for instance of the dark.

Sometimes in the evening Pauline would send me to fetch something from a distant room; she would take no refusal, and she was quite right, for otherwise I should have become very nervous, whereas now it is difficult to frighten me.

Thérèse later realized that this was an act of love by Pauline, in that Pauline sensed a certain nervousness or fear in Thérèse that she wanted her to overcome. By being gentle but firm in sending her to a distant room in the evening, Thérèse's little character was strengthened and she conquered her fears.

Reflection: Our love of others must lead us to see their needs. Authentic love will also show us the way by which we will help them to grow in the way they need to grow. Attentiveness to the details in the lives of others and prudence to know how to help them grow are central virtues in a relationship of love.

Oftentimes, in the midst of relationships, loved ones' weaknesses and faults may become very noticeable to you. When you see the faults of others, how do you respond to them? Do you act with criticism, anger or disgust? Or do you lovingly look for ways to help them grow in virtue?

Reflect, today, upon those closest to you and especially upon the weaknesses they have. Reflect also upon how God may want you to help them overcome those weaknesses so as to obtain the holiness God wants of them.

Dearest Saint Thérèse, you were greatly blessed by a motherly sister who helped you overcome your childish fear. Pauline taught you with gentleness, prudence and firmness, and you responded with openness.

Pray for me, that I may also respond to the guidance others give to me. Pray that I may always know how to guide others in the gentle ways of God. Saint Thérèse, pray for us.

Lesson Twenty-Four — The Happiness of the Saints

Lesson: Thérèse confided everything within her soul to her sister, Pauline. Most often, their conversations were deeply spiritual in nature, pondering together the great mysteries of their shared faith. Thérèse speaks about one such conversation:

> One day I expressed surprise that God does not give an equal amount of glory to all the elect in Heaven—I was afraid that they would not all be quite happy.

Pauline explained to Thérèse her understanding of the fullness of joy that each saint receives in Heaven by asking Thérèse to compare the difference between a thimble and a large glass. Pauline filled each one to the top with water and then asked Thérèse which one was fuller. Thérèse replied that they each were as full as the other. Pauline then explained that the same is true with the saints in Heaven. Each saint in Heaven is full of grace and, therefore, each saint was perfectly happy. Thérèse understood from this lesson that the least of the saints in Heaven do not envy the greatest, because each saint enjoys the fullness of God to the extent that each one's soul is capable.

This lesson brought the great mysteries of God down to the simple mind of Thérèse. This lesson also teaches that, while here on Earth, we each have the ability to grow in merit before God and, thus, to increase our Heavenly reward. While all saints in Heaven enjoy perfect joy, some have a greater capacity to shine forth with the beauty of God on account of the lives they lived on Earth. This should motivate us to seek greatness now so that our souls will be stretched to the greatest extent possible, enabling us to be eternally filled with the presence of God to the greatest extent.

Reflection: As you think of Heaven, do you desire to become the greatest of saints?   Or are you satisfied with becoming the least of saints?   It's true that every saint is filled with perfect joy, but it's also true that we determine our capacity for that fullness here and now as we journey through life.

Reflect upon this dual focus we must have.   First, we must strive to be saints.   But second, we are invited to become *great* saints.   Choose both of these goals today, and your reward in Heaven will be great.

Dearest Saint Thérèse, the capacity of your soul to contain the presence of God grew exponentially as you journeyed through life.   In Heaven, you are truly among the great saints of God.   Pray for me, that I may also imitate your burning love of God and thus grow in my capacity to be filled with His glorious presence.   Saint Thérèse, pray for us.

Lesson Twenty-Five — A Trial to Come

Lesson: When Thérèse was a child, God gave her a vivid vision of her father in an incapacitated state. In this vision, she saw him as an old man, walking silently with a veiled face through the forest. Thérèse called out to him in this vision, but he did not answer. The vision was so real to her that she convinced her sisters to go into the forest to look for their father so as to understand why he looked the way he did.

Though Thérèse's vision remained a mystery to her as a child, later in life this vision did come true. At age sixty-six, Thérèse's father suffered from two strokes and then suffered from paralysis for the next five years, three of those years in a hospital and the final two at home where he was cared for by two of his daughters.

Thérèse never forgot this vision she had of her father when she was but a child. Later in life, she continually pondered its meaning.

> "Why did God give this light to a child who, if she had understood it, would have died of grief?" "Why?" Here is one of those incomprehensible mysteries which we shall only understand in Heaven, where they will be the subject of our eternal admiration. My God, how good Thou art! How well dost Thou suit the trial to our strength!

One important lesson from this situation is that not everything God does in this life will make sense to us. Some things are to remain "incomprehensible mysteries" until we discover their meaning and purpose in Heaven. But we can be assured that when we do get to Heaven, every mystery we experience in this life will be made clear and will become the cause of our joy and admiration of God.

Reflection: Is there something in your life that remains an "incomprehensible mystery" to you? Perhaps something has happened to you or to a loved one, and you feel quite certain that God has permitted it, but you know not why. Or perhaps there is some other aspect of your life, or the life of a loved one, that has left you puzzled and even confused.

As you reflect upon your own mysteries of life, examine also if you are able to imitate Thérèse's faith and be content with knowing that some things will only be fully understood in Heaven. Too often we want everything to be made clear to us, but this is not always God's will. Sometimes God wants certain mysteries of life to remain so until Heaven. This cannot affect your faith negatively, rather, it must be the cause of much deeper trust in the providence and wisdom of our Almighty God.

Dearest Saint Thérèse, your faith was pure and strong, yet some things remained a mystery to you. As you encountered the mysteries of life, you grew in trust and admiration of God whose wisdom is beyond the human mind. Pray for me, that when I encounter the mysteries of life, I will respond with deep faith and abandonment to the unfathomable wisdom of God. Saint Thérèse, pray for us.

Lesson Twenty-Six — A Pretty Little Girl

Lesson: When Thérèse was six or seven, she saw the ocean for the first time. While at the beach, Thérèse overheard a man and a woman tell Mr. Martin that Thérèse was pretty. Thérèse had never heard this about herself before and was, at first, delighted to hear it. But she quickly dismissed those comments.

> My sisters were most careful never to talk before me in such a way as to spoil my simplicity and childish innocence; and, because I believed so implicitly in them, I attached little importance to the admiration of these people and thought no more about it.

It's an interesting contrast to consider. Was it better that Thérèse soaked in the comment about her being pretty? Or was it better to be more attentive to her sisters who did not ever talk to her in that way? It's quite common to speak of a child as being pretty, adorable or cute. But is it helpful to draw attention to this in the child's hearing? Some may believe that these statements are necessary so as to build up a child's self-confidence. But that's the key. Thérèse's sisters were not interested in helping Thérèse to become *self*-confident, becoming overly attentive to her external appearance. Rather, they chose to overlook this more superficial characteristic and to instead focus upon the deeper and more important truths of Thérèse's precious soul. Thérèse, for her part, having such an implicit trust in her sisters, would have easily been persuaded to become attentive to her external appearance in the eyes of others had her sisters regularly made this their focus.

A difficult lesson for many to learn, including parents, is that being pretty, or not so pretty, is of no consequence. We must seek to look beyond the mere externals and place all our focus upon the soul. Where there is sin, that sin must be gently addressed. Where there is virtue, that virtue must be nurtured so that it can grow. It is this form of subtle attentiveness to the most important characteristics in life that helps others grow in holiness.

Reflection: How much attention do you give to externals which are, in the end, of no eternal consequence? It's understandable that we are concerned about how we look. There is no sin in seeing one's exterior beauty. However, there is much greater virtue in being attentive only to the beauty of one's soul.

Reflect, today, upon how focused you are on the mere superficial aspects of life. Reflect, also, upon your conversations with others, especially children. Examine your conversations and commit yourself to an imitation of Thérèse's sisters who kept their eyes on the true beauty of their sister.

Dearest Saint Thérèse, you were blessed with sisters who saw your true beauty in your virtues and the grace of God at work in your precious soul. Pray for me, that I may keep my eyes on the beauty that is eternal and be unconcerned about that which is fleeting in this world. May I also be attentive to that true beauty in others so as to imitate the holy care of your loving sisters. Saint Thérèse, pray for us.

Chapter Three

Pauline Enters the Carmel

Lesson Twenty-Seven — Seeking Refuge

Lesson: When Thérèse was eight years old, she went to school at the Benedictine Abbey of Lisieux. She was one of the youngest girls there but also one of the brightest. As a result, she would often be teased and mistreated.

> Naturally timid and sensitive, I did not know how to defend myself, and could only cry in silence. Céline and my elder sisters did not know of my grief, and,

not being advanced enough in virtue to rise above these troubles, I suffered considerably.

The only way that Thérèse could deal with this difficulty at school was to take refuge at home every evening. There, she found the love she needed to lift her spirits and to endure the difficulties she faced at school.

Indeed, to be spoilt was a real necessity for me. The Little Flower had need to strike its tender roots deeper and deeper into the dearly loved garden of home, for nowhere else could it find the nourishment it required.

Her home was her refuge. As she grew and matured as a child, she allowed the love she received from her father and sisters to help her face the teasing she endured at school.

Reflection: We all need a place of refuge. Some will encounter similar difficulties as a child, and all of us, no matter our age or circumstance in life, will face various obstacles and sufferings. No matter the cause of our daily sufferings, and no matter the magnitude, we all need to discover the place of refuge where God can minister to our needs.

What is it in life that you endure, perhaps even on a daily basis, that causes you grief, sorrow or confusion? Perhaps you regularly experience some form of mistreatment as Thérèse did. Or perhaps you suffer from abuse to an even greater degree.

Look honestly at what causes the most difficulty in life and know that, even if it continues, God wants to offer you a place of refuge. Prayer, be it at church or in the solitude of your home, is one of the greatest places of refuge and consolation. Family and friends also often offer us a place for healing, clarity of mind and love.

Allow God to minister to you so that, like Thérèse, you will be able to daily sink the tender roots of your soul into the garden of God's love.

Dearest Saint Thérèse, your home was your refuge and garden of love. It was there that you found rich soil to nourish you as you encountered the ordinary sufferings of life. Pray for me, that I may also find the "garden" God gives me in which I can be nourished by the tender love and mercy of God. Saint Thérèse, pray for us.

Lesson Twenty-Eight — The Imagination of a Child

Lesson: Most children have wonderful imaginations and can spend hours playing and pretending to be someone they admire or hope to become. They may play house, imagining themselves to be parents, or, as it was with Thérèse and her cousin Marie Guérin, they regularly imagined themselves being religious hermits, seeking deep holiness of life.

Healthy imagination can easily inspire and motivate us toward the good and toward a life of virtue. It can also teach us many lessons in life as we ponder various mysteries of the lives of those we dream about. As Thérèse and Marie imagined themselves being austere hermits, living lives of prayer, solitude, poverty and penance, their little minds were formed and they daily engaged the mysteries of this holy vocation with fun and excitement.

Reflection: Perhaps you no longer spend time playing as a child does, but most people regularly find themselves in an imaginative world, daydreaming about greater things. What is it that you daydream about?

Some will find that they daydream about worldly endeavors: riches, popularity, success and the like. Others may daydream about less enjoyable activities such as revenge for a hurt received. Your imagination is important and is often the "playground" of the evil one. But it can also be the playground for the Holy Spirit to teach you and form you in holiness.

Reflect, today, upon all your usual daily reflections. Know that the imagination is a powerful tool that greatly influences you. Therefore, try to conform your daydreams only to a life of holiness in imitation of the saints. Allow the Holy Spirit to take over your imagination and to teach you many holy lessons, inspiring you to act in virtue and grace.

Dearest Saint Thérèse, like any ordinary little girl, you engaged in daily fun and play. You allowed your imagination to draw you into games imitating the holy hermits and into a life of virtue. Pray for me, that I may guard my imagination from the evil one and allow only God to inspire me so as to use this gift of reflection to grow into the saint I am called to become. Saint Thérèse, pray for us.

Lesson Twenty-Nine — The Greatest Day is Today!

Lesson: When Céline was eleven, she began her preparation for First Holy Communion. At the time, Thérèse was only seven and would not be able to make her First Holy Communion for four more years.

In the final weeks prior to Céline's receiving our Lord in the precious Sacrament, she vigorously prepared for this grace. Every evening her older sisters would sit her down and teach her about this special gift from God. One evening, as Thérèse listened on from a distance, she heard someone tell her sister, "From the time of your First Communion you must begin an entirely new life." That was all Thérèse needed to hear. From that moment on, she decided that she would not wait for her own First Communion to "begin an entirely new life." She decided that she would make that choice on the day Céline made her First Communion.

Very often in life we resolve that we will do this or that in the future. We decide to change with promises that are never fulfilled. One key to fulfilling our resolutions is to do them now, today, and not wait for some future date.

When Thérèse watched Céline make her First Communion, Thérèse indeed made that a moment of conversion in her own life. She recalls that it was one of the most beautiful days of her life. She did not hesitate; she did not wait.

Reflection: What is it that you find yourself putting off until tomorrow? What change is God asking of you that you hesitate about? Reflect upon these words of wisdom that Thérèse overheard as Céline was being prepared for Holy Communion: "You must begin an entirely new life." If you have already received Holy Communion, and regularly do receive this precious gift, then today is the day!

As you ponder this question, think about what comes to mind regarding your need to change. Whatever comes to mind first, that is most likely the area of your life God wants you to surrender to Him. Do not hesitate. Resolve today, and again tomorrow and again each day of your life. Continually seek to make this day the beginning of an "entirely new life," and God will lead you down a most glorious and beautiful path.

Dearest Saint Thérèse, you did not wait to give your whole life to God. You seized every opportunity to begin again and to surrender all. Pray for me, that I may also begin anew today and every day of my life. May every day be as my First Communion. May God receive the gift of my life and lead me down the path He desires. Saint Thérèse, pray for us.

Lesson Thirty — A Sacrifice of Love

Lesson: When Thérèse was only nine, her "second mother," Pauline, entered Carmel. In writing about this day, Thérèse revealed the following:

> In the afternoon of that October day, 1882, behind the grating of the Carmel, I saw my beloved Pauline, now become Sister Agnes of Jesus. Oh, how much I suffered in that parlour!

She also speaks of the sacrifice this was for her and how, by the grace of God, she endured it:

> At that time I did not know the joy of sacrifice; I was weak—so weak that I look on it as a great grace that I was able to bear such a trial, one seemingly so much beyond my strength—and yet live.

Prior to Pauline's entrance into Carmel, Thérèse discerned that she also was being called by God to join her sister as a Carmelite nun. Pauline arranged for her to speak to the Reverend Mother about this and, though she was sympathetic to her desire, she informed Thérèse that she would also have to wait until she was sixteen years old, which was seven years away!

After Pauline entered Carmel, Thérèse came to realize that the feelings of loss were only growing deeper. When she and her family were able to visit Pauline, Thérèse had but a few minutes with her alone. She could no longer spend hours with her beloved second mother. No longer could she pour out every detail of her heart to her. No longer was she continually in her presence. Finally, upon realizing the depth of the sacrifice she was enduring, she cried out to herself, "Pauline is lost to me!"

Pauline entered Carmel in answer to the call of God in her life. It was her fidelity to this calling which also offered Thérèse the opportunity to make the sacrifice of her new mother to God. Because Thérèse loved Pauline so deeply, the sacrifice she was called to make was also very deep. But the deeper the love, the more powerful the sacrifice.

Reflection: What is God calling you to offer Him as a sacrifice of love? Do not be disillusioned into thinking that the will of God is always paved with a bed of roses. At its heart, love is sacrificial. It requires death to our own will and, at times, it requires we let go of all earthly attachments, even attachments that are pure and holy, such as the love shared by Thérèse and Pauline.

Ponder those circumstances in your life to which it is difficult to say "Yes." As you see the sacrifices God wants of you, do not be deterred from your "Yes" on account of the sacrifice involved. Know that Jesus paved the way by laying down His life in the ultimate and unlimited Sacrifice of Love. He also calls us to do the same.

Dearest Saint Thérèse, you felt the pain of the sacrifice God was asking of you when He called your beloved second mother and dear sister, Pauline, to enter into the walls of Carmel. Your suffering was on account of your love and that God asked much of you. Pray for me, that I may love so deeply that God asks me for the ultimate sacrifice of my life. May I imitate the perfect "Yes" of our Blessed Mother and Jesus Himself by the help of your prayers. Saint Thérèse, pray for us.

Lesson Thirty-One — Our Lady of Victories!

Lesson: Thérèse's pain at the departure of her dear Pauline to Carmel was so great that she became seriously ill. It was as if the evil one was furious at Pauline's entrance into Carmel and did not want Thérèse to follow her.

Physical manifestations of her pain started one day when she was with her aunt and uncle. Thérèse began to shake and experience tremors, and there was little that could be done. The family doctor could not give a diagnosis, but another doctor stated that Thérèse was experiencing serious neurological episodes on account of her extreme emotional distress.

As the illness went on for months, her family was very concerned. Pauline wrote her many letters from Carmel, her father did all he could for her and her sisters were always at her side. At times she was delirious, at times unresponsive and at times she would temporarily recover.

One day, Louis asked his daughter Marie to take some gold coins to the shrine of Our Lady of Victories in Paris to have a novena of Masses said for Thérèse. Prayer was now the only answer and a miracle the only cure. Shortly after that, Thérèse lay on her bed, still delirious and confused. Her three sisters all knelt before a statue of the Blessed Mother that was set up for Thérèse to see. Thérèse also prayed and later wrote about what she experienced:

> Suddenly the statue seemed to come to life and grow beautiful, with a divine beauty that I shall never find words to describe. The expression of Our Lady's face was ineffably sweet, tender, and compassionate; but what touched me to the very depths of my soul was her gracious smile. Then, all my pain vanished, two big tears started to my eyes and fell silently.

Thérèse was cured! Our Lady had worked a miracle for her, but it was more than a physical healing. Thérèse also discovered much joy at her dear Pauline's vocation:

> My first visit there after my illness was full of joy at seeing Pauline clothed in the habit of Our Lady of Carmel. It was a happy time for us both, we had so much to say, we had both suffered so much. My heart was so full that I could hardly speak.

Thérèse no longer felt as though Pauline was lost to her. Our Lady cured her of this deep sorrow and began to prepare her for the wonderful journey ahead as she would soon enter Carmel herself.

Reflection: Have you ever allowed your emotions to overwhelm you to the point that you became ill as a result? Even if you have not experienced physical illness, you most likely have felt the ill effects of emotional distress, anxiety and the like.

Reflect upon the fact that God wants to free you from the anxieties of life. Our emotions are a powerful gift from God. They can be used for much love and can become a source of great devotion and drive in life. However, when they are not properly ordered, they can cause us many difficulties.

Reflect upon your emotions and distresses this day. Offer them to our Blessed Mother and trust in her intercession. Even the greatest saints, like little Thérèse, need the intercession of our Lady of Victories in their lives.

Dearest Saint Thérèse, you loved your sister Pauline with such a love that her departure was too much to bear. But the love of your family and the intercession of Our Lady of Victories brought you joy and healing. Pray for me, that the pains and sorrows I feel in life will be healed by God so that I may embrace His holy will with much joy. Saint Thérèse, pray for us.

Chapter Four

First Communion and Confirmation

Lesson Thirty-Two — "The Little Flower of the Divine Prisoner"

Lesson: As a child, Thérèse was like a sponge waiting to soak up all she perceived. Fortunately, she was surrounded with wonderful influences from the earliest age. Her sister Pauline, one of the most influential persons in her life, used to teach Thérèse about faith in many ways. One such way was through the use of holy pictures.

> I owe some of the happiest and strongest impressions which have encouraged me in the practice of virtue to the beautiful pictures Pauline used to show me. Everything was forgotten while looking at them.

One image that affected Thérèse profoundly was the image of "The Little Flower of the Divine Prisoner." In this image, Jesus is depicted as a prisoner, looking out of His cell through a barred window at a single white flower placed on the ledge of the window. The prison was meant to depict the Tabernacle containing the divine presence of our Lord. The little white flower was to depict the consolation given to Jesus every time He was visited in the Tabernacle.

Thérèse spent much time meditating upon this image, "gazing at it in a kind of ecstasy." Through her meditation, Thérèse grew in a desire to be that "Little Flower" outside the cell of Jesus, consoling Him in His imprisoned state.

> I offered myself to Our Lord to be His Little Flower; I longed to console Him, to draw as near as possible to the Tabernacle, to be looked on, cared for, and gathered by Him.

It was this image that stood out to Thérèse above all because it was a clear depiction of the vocation she was called to embrace. She would one day enter the "prison" of the Carmelite convent and would be locked behind the grate with other holy nuns. Within this prison of love, she would be that Little Flower who consoled the Heart of Jesus by her love and adoration.

Reflection: You, too, are called to console the Heart of Jesus as He remains imprisoned within the Tabernacle and in so many other hidden ways. When you are at church, before the Tabernacle, do you make acts of love so as to console our Lord? The simplest act of love would be to kneel before the Tabernacle and say to our Lord, "I love You." Doing so will allow you to be another little flower offered to Him by your faith.

Seek to find Jesus in your midst. Find Him, love Him, adore and console Him. In doing so, you will also participate in the beautiful vocation of Saint Thérèse, God's Little Flower.

Dearest Saint Thérèse, God's Little Flower, you discovered your vocation to console the Heart of Jesus and you embraced it with all your heart. Pray for me, that I may imitate you and continue this beautiful vocation you were given. May I discover the Divine Prisoner all around me and love Him with all my heart. Saint Thérèse, pray for us.

Lesson Thirty-Three — "I Shall Become a Great Saint"

Lesson: As Sister Thérèse reflected upon her childhood and upon her time as a Carmelite nun, she continually sensed that one day she would be a great saint. She was aware of the fact that this sense may appear to be rash, since she knew she was far from perfect. Nonetheless, she stated clearly that she believed God would do this by His grace and not by her own effort.

> It is He alone, Who, pleased with my feeble efforts, will raise me to Himself, and, by clothing me with His merits, make me a Saint.

As a child, Thérèse enjoyed reading as her favorite pastime. She read about Joan of Arc and other venerable heroines of France as well as many other books chosen for her by her sisters. As she reflected upon the lives of those about whom she read, and how they were admired by many, she understood that her greatness would be different. Her greatness would be hidden during her life, even from her own eyes. It was this hiddenness that Sister Thérèse acknowledged as one of the greatest graces she received in life. Though she is now venerated as a great saint and her soul is on display through her writings for all to see, she was formed and nurtured in the secrecy of her heart, and it was within this interior sanctuary that God created so many beautiful virtues.

We are all called to become great saints, but we achieve this goal in varied ways. The virtues of some will be visible far and wide during their lives on earth. Others are called to greatness in a far more silent way, their virtue seen primarily by God. But in Heaven, the greatness of each saint will be manifest, and all will rejoice in the beautiful virtues bestowed on each by God.

Reflection: Do you want to become a great saint? The first step in becoming one is to desire it with all your heart.

The next step is to begin walking down the path of virtue, allowing God to transform your soul into the saint you are to become.

Ponder your call to sanctity and know that it is a goal that you can achieve. Let God decide the path for your life and seek to discover it every day. Do not covet the holiness of others or envy the vocation they have been given. Seek only the path chosen for you and resolutely determine to journey down that path toward Heaven.

Dearest Saint Thérèse, God formed greatness in you in a hidden way. You lived a quiet life with your family and continued that solitude within the walls of the Carmelite convent. But in your hiddenness, great things were taking place within your soul. Pray for me, that I may seek only the path of holiness God has laid out before me. May I become a great saint and rejoice in that fact forever in Heaven. Saint Thérèse, pray for us.

Lesson Thirty-Four — The Charm of the World

Lesson: After Thérèse had been cured of her childhood illness, her father lavished much attention on her and began to show her many parts of the world she had not yet seen and to meet many new people. She acknowledged that she was "petted, made much of, admired" and that for a period of two weeks after her illness her "path was strewn with flowers."

She discovered that part of her was attracted to all this attention and that many people seemed to live for this form of charm that the world offers.

> At ten years of age the heart is easily fascinated, and I confess that in my case this kind of life had its charms. Alas! the world knows well how to combine its pleasures with the service of God.

But Thérèse did not allow herself to become seduced by worldly "joys" and realized that these pleasures were passing, not eternal. The compliments, small talk, pleasures, worldly esteem and earthly successes were superficial and deceptive when made an end in themselves. Thérèse understood that Heaven is the only joy to seek in life and the only satisfaction that is eternal.

Reflection: How attracted are you to worldly seductions? The world's charms existed before TV and mass media culture, as Thérèse realized even as a child. Moreover, advertisements, TV shows and other forms of communication today present to us subtle but very influential images of what true happiness is all about. It is difficult to remain free of these many influences and charms and to keep our eyes on the true joys given to us by God.

Ponder your desires and attraction to worldly success, praise, admiration and the like. If you are successful, praised or admired in the world, this is fine. But desiring these superficial charms and making them the "joys" that you live for is dangerous.

Seek the joys and rewards of Heaven alone. Making this choice is a choice you will never regret.

Dearest Saint Thérèse, you had your eyes fixed on Heaven and understood that Heaven was the only source of eternal joy. You did not allow yourself to become seduced by the passing pleasures of this world, choosing instead the pleasures that were eternal. Pray for me, that I may also keep my eyes on the one joy that matters in life. May I do the will of God in all things and find joy in this alone. Saint Thérèse, pray for us.

Lesson Thirty-Five — Preparing for Jesus

Lesson: Little Thérèse received her First Holy Communion on May 8, 1884 at the age of eleven. She had hoped to receive it a year earlier but missed the age requirement by only a few days. She sought a dispensation but was not able to receive it. So she waited.

The three months prior to Thérèse's First Communion were filled with preparation in the most beautiful, thoughtful, meticulous and prayerful of ways. Her preparation became a mission engaged in by her whole family, especially her sisters Pauline and Marie. Her preparations were lovingly recorded in many letters written during those three months, especially letters written by her second mother, Pauline, who was now Sister Agnes of Jesus.

Sister Agnes prepared a lovely *"little book* of preparation" for Thérèse that included beautiful prayers, meditations and lessons by which little Thérèse could devoutly prepare her soul for this most glorious meeting with her little Jesus. In her diary, Sister Thérèse wrote the following:

> I shall always remember my First Communion Day as one of unclouded happiness. It seems to me that I could not have been better prepared. Do you remember, dear Mother, the charming little book you gave me three months before the great day? I found in it a helpful method which prepared me gradually and thoroughly.

While Sister Agnes prepared Thérèse from the convent through the little book of preparation and by weekly letters about Holy Communion, her sister Marie prepared Thérèse from home:

> I had Marie, too, who took Pauline's place. Every evening I spent a long time with her, listening eagerly to all she said. How delightfully she talked to me! I felt myself set on fire by her noble, generous spirit.

Thérèse understood well the importance of her First Holy Communion and did not squander her time in preparation for this most precious gift. Her preparation paid off and her First Communion day was one filled with the greatest blessings.

Reflection: Even if it has been many years since you made your First Communion, do you remember it? Who helped you prepare to receive Jesus in the Most Holy Sacrament of the Eucharist? Did you feel well-prepared to receive him? What was special about that day?

Preparation for First Communion is really preparation for every Communion we receive. Our preparation must be ongoing. Ponder the question from this perspective: How well do you prepare your soul for the ongoing gift of Jesus in this glorious Sacrament? Do you regularly ponder the reality of God coming to you in this hidden, mysterious and profound way? Do you pray, meditate, make sacrifices and confess your sins regularly so that every Communion you receive is as if it were your first?

Ponder, this day, the three months of intense spiritual preparation Thérèse engaged in with the help of her family and seek to imitate her desire to make her soul the most beautiful garden in which her little Jesus would plant the seeds of His Body, Blood, Soul and Divinity. Never cease preparing yourself for this glorious gift and do not fail to understand its importance.

Dearest Saint Thérèse, you lovingly prepared for the most glorious gift of the Precious Body and Blood of your Savior. You opened yourself to the many lessons your sisters taught you so that you could become a suitable dwelling place of your little Jesus. Pray for me, that I may continually prepare my soul for this precious gift every time I attend Mass and receive Holy Communion. May I imitate your preparedness and receive the same transforming graces you received. Saint Thérèse, pray for us.

Lesson Thirty-Six — Perfect Union

Lesson: After three months of preparation, the day of her First Communion was almost here. She spent the last few days at an abbey for retreat and continued her loving preparation. She received final instructions, listened attentively to the lessons taught by the priest, and prayed fervently as the great day arrived.

> At last there dawned the most beautiful day of all the days of my life. How perfectly I remember even the smallest details of those sacred hours! the joyful awakening, the reverent and tender embraces of my mistresses and older companions, the room filled with snow-white frocks, where each child was dressed in turn, and, above all, our entrance into the chapel and the melody of the morning hymn: "O Altar of God, where the Angels are hovering."

Thérèse was overwhelmed with love on this "most beautiful day of all the days" of her life. She later described her experience by stating, "one's inmost thoughts cannot be translated into earthly words without instantly losing their deep and heavenly meaning." But despite the inability to translate her experience into words, Thérèse described her First Communion as best she could:

> How sweet was the first embrace of Jesus! It was indeed an embrace of love. I felt that I was loved, and I said: "I love Thee, and I give myself to Thee for ever." ...That day our meeting was more than simple recognition, it was perfect union. We were no longer two. Thérèse had disappeared like a drop of water lost in the immensity of the ocean; Jesus alone remained—He was the Master, the King!

Upon receiving Holy Communion, Thérèse broke down in tears. As she cried, her friends did not understand. They wondered if Thérèse was sad that her mother was not there or if she had something for which she felt guilty. They did not realize how deeply she and her little Jesus loved each other and how deeply He transformed her precious soul.

> Night came, and so ended that beautiful day. Even the brightest days are followed by darkness; one alone will know no setting, the day of the First and Eternal Communion in our true Home. Somehow the next day seemed sorrowful. The pretty clothes and the presents I had received could not satisfy me. Henceforth Our Lord alone could fill my heart, and all I longed for was the blissful moment when I should receive Him again.

Reflection: Few people have prepared so well, and loved Jesus so deeply, so as to enter into perfect union with Jesus as they receive Him in Holy Communion. This "divine fusion" as it has also been called must become the central goal of all of our lives. How deeply have you entered into union with our Lord when you received Him in Holy Communion?

Thérèse's experience of oneness with Jesus, being as a single drop of water that is plunged into a mighty ocean, is what we will experience forever in Heaven. If you are willing, God wants you to begin this oneness now. Reflect upon this powerful imagery from a little child. Allow her experience, including her tears, to teach you and to inspire you to allow your reception of this glorious Sacrament to transform your life.

Dearest Saint Thérèse, you were overwhelmed and filled with the utmost joy as your precious Jesus entered your soul in the Blessed

Sacrament for the very first time. Pray for me, that I may learn from what you experienced and seek to embrace Him ever more deeply in my life. May the Most Blessed Sacrament, our Divine Lord Himself, always find the perfect home within my soul. May Jesus and I truly become one. Saint Thérèse, pray for us.

Lesson Thirty-Seven — I Live Now, Not I

Lesson: After her First Communion, Thérèse longed to receive Jesus again and again. She made her second Communion on Ascension Day, kneeling between her father and Marie. Once again, she broke down in tears as she prayed fervently, uniting her soul with her Jesus in perfect union.

> I kept repeating those words of St. Paul: "I live now, not I; but Christ liveth in me." After this second visit of Our Lord I longed for nothing else but to receive Him.

In those days, Holy Communion was reserved for very special feasts. Thérèse would look forward to each feast day, and her sister Marie would always prepare her the night before so that she was ready each time she received Jesus in the Sacred Host.

Thérèse lived on a different level than most girls her age. Her depth and insights into the divine mysteries were beyond what the normal human mind can fathom. Little by little, her precious Jesus, who now regularly came to her in Holy Communion, began to teach her and to guide her down the road of permanent union. Thérèse also began to discover that this road led to the sufferings of Jesus' holy Cross.

Reflection: Have you ever had the experience of Jesus living within you? Do the words Thérèse prayed in imitation of Saint Paul: "I live now, not I; but Christ liveth in me," ever resound within your own heart?

Reflect, today, upon the invitation God gives you to become deeply united with Him through prayer and the Sacraments, so that you, like Thérèse, will speak those words naturally and easily. Divine union is the sole purpose of life and must become your singular focus in life.

Dearest Saint Thérèse, you were in awe of Jesus as you received Him in Holy Communion time and time again. He continued to transform you and to lead you down the road that He walked. Pray for me, that I may seek to walk the same road of sanctity and will be perfectly united to Jesus now and for eternity. Saint Thérèse, pray for us.

Lesson Thirty-Eight — Fortitude in Suffering

Lesson: Early on, Thérèse grew in a desire for suffering and longed to embrace all suffering as a sacrifice made with love. Holy Communion nourished this desire within her soul, and she began to have great consolation at the thought of it, even if she did not yet understand how much she would suffer.

> During my thanksgiving after Holy Communion I often repeated this passage from the Imitation of Christ: "O my God, who art unspeakable sweetness,

turn for me into bitterness all the consolations of earth."

Soon after her First Communion, Thérèse began preparing for the full outpouring of the Holy Spirit in the Sacrament of Confirmation. She prepared beautifully, just as she did for her First Communion. When the day came, she was given a special gift that would help her fulfill her vocation of suffering.

> I did not feel the mighty wind of the first Pentecost, but rather the gentle breeze which the prophet Elias heard on Mount Horeb. On that day I received the gift of fortitude in suffering—a gift I needed sorely, for the martyrdom of my soul was soon to begin.

In those days, Thérèse did not suffer much. Even then, Jesus was preparing her for the day when she would cry out on her deathbed, "Oh! It's pure suffering because there are no consolations! No, not one!...No, I would never have believed that one could suffer so much...Never! Never!" But for now, this little queen began to grow in virtue and wisdom so that she could one day follow her Lord to Calvary.

Reflection: Ponder, today, the apparent contradiction of union with Christ and suffering. They go hand in hand while on this Earth because it was suffering that God used to redeem the world. This is no easy lesson to learn!

Just as little Thérèse began to gain spiritual insight into the joy of suffering, seek to discover this same spiritual mystery. Seek to discover Christ on the Cross and know that through your communion with Him, He will use your suffering to transform your life. Pray, also, for the gift of Fortitude so that you, like Thérèse, will be able to endure the Cross with Christ.

Saint Thérèse, it was through the Sacraments of Holy Communion and Confirmation that you began to discover the mystery of suffering and your martyrdom. Pray for me, that I may also understand the suffering I endure and may come to see it as a glorious means to Heaven. May I receive the same gift of fortitude that you received and carry my cross with courage and strength. Saint Thérèse, pray for us.

Lesson Thirty-Nine — True Friendship

Lesson: After Thérèse received First Communion and Confirmation, she returned to her day school at the Abbey and resumed her lessons. She excelled in catechism class but struggled with other subjects.

On the playground, Thérèse attempted to forge new friendships with little success. She did make friends with two girls but found that these friendships were not very fulfilling.

> One of them had to stay at home for some months; while she was away I thought about her very often, and on her return I showed how pleased I was. However, all I got was a glance of indifference—my friendship was not appreciated. I felt this very keenly, and I no longer sought an affection which had proved so inconstant. Nevertheless I still love my little school friend, and continue to pray for her,

for God has given me a faithful heart, and when once I love, I love for ever.

Thérèse's experience of friendship with the girls at school is telling of what she hoped for and even expected in a friendship. Sadly, many children never experience the depth of love and affection that Thérèse experienced from her parents and her sisters. Thérèse learned from her family that friendship shared between those who love God deeply and love each other deeply was exceptionally rewarding. When Thérèse sought a similar relationship of love with the girls at school and could not find it, she thought, "How shallow are the hearts of creatures!"

It's not that the other girls at school were different, it was that Thérèse was different. She knew what it meant to love and be loved to a profound degree. She not only enjoyed the deepest of love as it was expressed within her family, she also knew what it was like to be perfectly in love with God. Her heart was so well formed that, try as she may, she could not find this depth of love among her classmates.

Reflection: How deeply have you loved and been loved by another? We certainly must love God with all our might, and God unquestionably loves us with a perfect love. But we do not always allow that love to consume us so that we can understand the depth of His love. As for the love of others, what a gift it is to discover a soul who loves you with the deepest and most holy love!

Reflect upon your own experience of love. Start with the love of God. After you ponder the love you give and receive from God, look also at your human relationships.

Are they more superficial and shallow, or have you been blessed with true friends with whom your heart has been deeply united?

Thérèse and her sisters, when they were apart from each other, would write many letters. They always ended their letters by saying, "I love you and I kiss you with all my heart." And they meant it. Pray that you may also be blessed to know such holy love.

Dearest Saint Thérèse, you, your sisters and your parents shared a bond of love that few others know. It was a bond of selfless and pure love centered in the love of God. Pray for me, that I may know how to lavish love upon others with all my heart. Pray that God will send true friends into my life, that I may know of His love and affection through them. Saint Thérèse, pray for us.

Lesson Forty — Preserved from Sin by Mercy

Lesson: Thérèse had much admiration for saints such as Saint Mary Magdalene who, though grave sinners, manifested great repentance in their lives. She often heard it said that grave sinners who repented loved God more than those who never lost their baptismal innocence. Thérèse firmly disagreed with those words!

She realized, at an early age, that the Father had been so merciful to her that He preserved her from falling into grave sin. When she made a general confession to her spiritual director at age fifteen, the priest told her that she had never committed a mortal sin. Thérèse continued in a state of grace throughout her life. But she knew this was not to her merit. She knew that this grace, which preserved her from grave sin, was on account of God's mercy. As a result, Thérèse was even more grateful to God and loved Him with a greater love than some who had been forgiven much. It was her realization of what she was *preserved* from that compelled her to such gratitude and love of God.

Reflection: It's true that those who have been forgiven much are often filled with gratitude for the forgiveness they have received. But do we have to wait until we fall into sin and repent to be filled with gratitude and love of God?

Look into your own heart and ponder how grateful you are to God for His mercy. If you find that your love and gratitude are, at best, lukewarm, ponder why. Most likely it is because you have not properly understood how much God has done in your life. Don't wait until you need forgiveness to be grateful to God. Like Thérèse, discover how much God has already done for you and from how much He has preserved you. Only by understanding this truth will you be able to grow in gratitude and love of Him who is Love and Mercy itself.

Dearest Saint Thérèse, though you were never in need of the mercy given to those who sin mortally, you were nonetheless aware of how abundantly merciful God had been to you. By preserving you from grave sin, God forgave you everything! Pray for me, that I may understand how much God has done for me. May I never lack gratitude and grow daily in greater love of our glorious God. Saint Thérèse, pray for us.

Lesson Forty-One — Scruples

Lesson: Thérèse was not perfect. Though she had never fallen into mortal sin, she did struggle with a serious case of scruples.

> It was during the retreat before my second Communion that I was attacked by the terrible disease of scruples. One must have passed through this martyrdom to understand it. It would be quite impossible for me to tell you what I suffered for nearly two years.

Scruples is a spiritual struggle in which a person becomes obsessed with sin and one's own perceived moral failings to a dangerous degree. Some psychologists identify this moral struggle as a spiritual form of Obsessive Compulsive Disorder. Those who struggle with scruples cannot look at their sins clearly, in the light of God's mercy. Every perceived weakness or sin is magnified and becomes a terrible burden, causing anxiety and fear.

Eventually, Thérèse's scruples made her so sick that she had to leave school at the age of thirteen. Her extremely sensitive nature and her desire for perfection began to confuse her thinking and she would cry every time she was aware of the least imperfection.

For example, on one occasion her aunt gave her a blue ribbon for her hair. At first, she was delighted with it. But soon, her scruples got the best of her and she began to believe that putting this blue ribbon in her hair was nothing other than vanity. "But this childish pleasure seemed sinful to me, and I had so many scruples that I had to go to Confession, even at Trouville."

During this period of almost two years, Thérèse continually poured out her soul to her sister Marie who listened to her with much patience. Marie became her earthly confidant and guide through this dark struggle. However, before this struggle with scruples was ended, Marie entered Carmel, and Thérèse no longer had anyone on Earth to whom she could pour out her heart. Therefore, she began to speak to her four little siblings who were in Heaven. Thérèse confided everything to these "little angels"' and their prayers for Thérèse were eventually answered. Thérèse began to find freedom from her scruples as she came to understand how much these four little angels loved her from Heaven and prayed for her.

Reflection: Do you struggle with scruples? It seems that most people struggle not with scrupulosity but with a dull conscience and fail to see their sin as God sees it. For those who do struggle with scrupulosity, their cross is difficult to bear.

Scrupulosity is a failure to see sin in the light of God's perfect mercy. We are all sinful, and for that reason, we are all offered the unfathomable gift of the mercy of God. God is most generous with His mercy, and we must acknowledge that mercy as we acknowledge our sins.

Reflect upon how clearly you see your sin in the light of God's mercy, and know that God loves you with a perfect love. Seeing your sin in this way will not weigh you down.

Rather, it will enable you to be freed of your sin and to rejoice in the goodness of God.

Dearest Saint Thérèse, you carried a heavy burden of scrupulosity for almost two years. With time and grace, you were freed from this struggle and began to understand God's love for you in a new light. Pray for me, that I may always see my sin clearly and that I may also understand God's perfect mercy. May I open my heart to that mercy and overcome my sin with confidence and courage. Saint Thérèse, pray for us.

Chapter Five

Vocation of Thérèse

Lesson Forty-Two — A Christmas Miracle

Lesson: Though the prayers of her "little angels" (her siblings in Heaven) began to alleviate Thérèse's scruples, she had not fully rid herself of her extreme sensitivity and knew she needed a miracle. This miracle took place on Christmas Day, 1886, just nine days before Thérèse's fourteenth birthday.

> On that blessed night the sweet Infant Jesus, scarce an hour old, filled the darkness of my soul with floods of light. By becoming weak and little, for love of me, He made me strong and brave; He put His own weapons into my hands, so that I went from victory to victory, beginning, if I may say so, "to run as a giant" (Cf. Psalm 18[19]:5). The fountain of my tears was dried up, and from that time they flowed neither easily nor often.

That Christmas night, Thérèse received the grace of a complete conversion. Though she had labored for years to overcome her extreme sensitivity and her tendency to cry over everything, she could not change her nature. But God could, and He did.

> On this night of grace, the third period of my life began—the most beautiful of all, the one most filled with heavenly favours. In an instant, Our Lord, satisfied with my good will, accomplished the work I had not been able to do during all these years.

Thérèse began to grow in fortitude and strength of character. Her sisters and her father were in awe of her sudden transformation and knew it was a true Christmas miracle. Thus, with this childish obstacle cured, Thérèse was now one step closer to being ready to fulfill her vocation as a Carmelite nun.

Reflection: Is there one struggle in your life that you have not been able to overcome, no matter how hard you tried? What is it that requires more than your own effort to achieve? What miracle do you need so as to achieve a "complete conversion?"

We all struggle and we all need grace. At times, there may be one particular struggle that causes us much grief. It might be a weakness within our nature, or it might be some burden imposed upon us that is beyond our control. What is your struggle?

Reflect upon the primary struggle in your life and acknowledge your powerlessness to overcome it. Only when you admit your weakness and abandon yourself fully to God, can God perform a miracle in your life.

Dearest Saint Thérèse, you struggled for years with the weakness of being overly sensitive and often cried at the slightest disturbance. Through your perseverance in prayer, God performed a miracle in you and freed you from this struggle. Pray for me, that I may recognize my powerlessness to overcome my struggles. May I turn to God in complete abandonment so as to obtain the complete conversion of my life. Saint Thérèse, pray for us.

Lesson Forty-Three — A Fisher of Souls

Lesson: After Thérèse's complete conversion, she entered her fourteenth year of life with a newfound love of sinners.

> From that day the cry of my dying Saviour—"I thirst!"—sounded incessantly in my heart, and kindled therein a burning zeal hitherto unknown to me. My one desire was to give my Beloved to drink; I felt myself consumed with thirst for souls, and I

longed at any cost to snatch sinners from the everlasting flames of hell.

Shortly after discovering this new thirst for sinners, Thérèse became aware of a notorious criminal named Pranzini who was soon to be executed for his crimes and who had shown no sign of repentance. Therefore, this new little apostle for sinners used "all the spiritual means" she could think of to bring about the conversion of Pranzini's soul. Though she was fully confident God would answer her prayer, she asked for a sign of his repentance, since this was her "first sinner."

> "My God, I am quite sure that Thou wilt pardon this unhappy Pranzini. I should still think so if he did not confess his sins or give any sign of sorrow, because I have such confidence in Thy unbounded Mercy; but this is my first sinner, and therefore I beg for just one sign of repentance to reassure me."

Sure enough, Thérèse received her sign. Just before his execution, despite the fact that he refused to confess his sins and receive absolution, the newspaper recorded that Pranzini, moved by what seemed to be a sudden inspiration just before death, embraced a crucifix held out by the priest and kissed it three times. Thérèse's prayers were answered, and she had won her first sinner for Heaven.

Reflection: What do you "thirst" for in life? Too often, we allow ourselves to be drawn to passing delights and selfish ambitions. We thirst for money, recognition, pleasure and more.

Thérèse came to understand that the only good thirst her soul should have was the thirst in the Heart of Jesus. As Jesus hung dying on the Cross, His thirst was for souls.

Reflect upon your own thirst, your cravings and your desires. Do you have the thirst within the heart of Christ? Do you thirst for the salvation of souls? Do you long to see God's mercy poured out in abundance upon every sinner? Or do you find yourself condemning the sinner as you remain stuck in your own self-righteousness?

Seek to imitate this desire in the heart of Jesus to the same extent that it was alive in the heart of little Thérèse and know that this thirst can only be satisfied by love. Pray for this gift and let God save many souls through you.

Dearest Saint Thérèse, your heart was filled with a longing to save sinners. The thirst of your soul was a beautiful sharing in the thirst of Jesus on the Cross. Pray for me, that I may also thirst for the salvation of souls. May God use me as He chooses to be an instrument of His mercy to the greatest sinner. Saint Thérèse, pray for us.

Lesson Forty-Four — A Time of Learning

Lesson: Now a girl of fourteen, Thérèse was maturing quickly. Her physical stature was changing, she was growing tall, and she discovered a newfound love for learning. All of this began with her Christmas miracle.

> Now that I was free from scruples and morbid sensitiveness, my mind developed. I had always

loved what was noble and beautiful, and about this time I was seized with a passionate desire for learning. Not content with lessons from my teachers, I took up certain subjects by myself, and learnt more in a few months than I had in my whole school life.

Up until this time, the only book that seemed to nourish Thérèse was the *Imitation of Christ*. However, after her Christmas conversion Thérèse began learning fervently in numerous ways. She read Father Charles Arminjon's *The End of this World and the Mysteries of the World to Come*. This book had a huge impact upon her. Every evening she and Céline would go up to the attic window together to gaze at the stars and engage in spiritual conversations from which she gained much wisdom and spiritual insight. Thérèse was also being taught directly by Jesus. It was as if she had a newfound gift of spiritual knowledge and learning.

As she matured physically and intellectually, she also grew in virtue. Thérèse began to make small daily sacrifices, which had the effect of increasing her virtue. Her prayer life deepened and she began to receive Holy Communion more often, even daily with the permission of her confessor. Thérèse realized: "[Jesus] does not come down from Heaven each day in order to remain in a golden ciborium, but to find another Heaven—the Heaven of our souls in which He takes such delight."

Little by little, Thérèse was maturing and receiving the necessary graces to enter the Carmelite convent at age fifteen. But if she were to be ready to enter Carmel within a year, God still had much work to do in her soul.

Reflection: God's ways are always perfect. Sometimes we go through painful and confusing periods in life, only to have these trials lifted so as to enter into new endeavors. God teaches us through books, conversations, prayer, daily experiences and sometimes by directly communicating to us in our soul.

In what way does God want you to be formed at this time in your life? Is He asking you to engage in greater sacrifice, to read and study, to show more charity, to increase your prayer? Though all of these are good, God will give special graces when we need them so as to be formed in the way we need at each moment of our lives.

Reflect upon the specific needs you have in your life right now, and examine your conscience to discern whether there is some gentle God-given invitation to which you must respond. Say "Yes" to whatever God wants to do in your soul, and you will be in awe of the joy you receive in following His perfect plan for your life.

Dearest Saint Thérèse, God did great things in your soul and provided all that you needed to prepare for your lovely vocation in the Carmel convent. Pray for me, that I may respond to the graces I am given to prepare my own soul for the work God has given only to me. May I imitate your willing cooperation with grace and grow in wisdom and virtue so that I may also be used in accord with the perfect will of God. Saint Thérèse, pray for us.

Lesson Forty-Five — Persevering to Carmel

Lesson: Even though Thérèse had desired to give herself entirely to God from the age of three, her desire and conviction continued to grow during her childhood and young adolescence. In reflecting upon this time in her life she thought, "The Divine Call was becoming so insistent that, had it been necessary for me to go through fire, I would have thrown myself into it to follow my Divine Master."

She spoke of her calling to Pauline and Céline, and they both offered wholehearted support. When she spoke to her father she did so through tears, both hers and his. He listened intently and understood that her desire to enter the convent was from God. With love, he offered his little Queen his blessing and support. Her uncle Isidore Guérin did not immediately agree that this was a good idea and told Thérèse that only a miracle would change his mind. However, shortly after that conversation, Thérèse's uncle again told her that he had prayed to God for knowledge of His perfect will and that God made it clear to him that this was Thérèse's calling. He ended their conversation by saying, "Go in peace, my dear child, you are a privileged little flower which Our Lord wishes to gather. I will put no obstacle in the way."

With her uncle's consent and that of her father and sisters, Thérèse set her eyes and heart on the vocation to which she was being called. However, she soon met a roadblock when the Ecclesiastical Superior of the Carmelites, Canon Delatroette, would not allow Thérèse to enter until she was twenty-one years of age. He worried that she was only following in the footsteps of her sister and that hers was not a true vocation. She and her father met with him, but he was insistent. Although this meeting left Thérèse with much sorrow, she did not lose hope, since the Superior also said that she was welcome to seek permission directly from the Bishop, which she immediately resolved to do.

Reflection: At times, it seems as though God's will is impossible to fulfill. Obstacles often arise along the way, and those who are easily discouraged are quickly dissuaded. But obstacles are often permitted by God to deepen our resolve to follow Him with unwavering commitment.

What obstacles do you find in your life that keep you from fulfilling the will of God in your life? What is your reaction to these obstacles? It's easy to give in to despair and to allow these "tests" of our endurance to wear us down.

Reflect upon the simple truth that whatever God is calling you to do in life, He will provide you with the means of achieving it. No matter how great or small the calling, our perseverance is essential. If there is something that is deterring you from fulfilling the will of God in your life, try to look at it from a new perspective. See every obstacle as a gift by which God wants to strengthen you and deepen your commitment to His will. Grow stronger and do not waver from the gentle but clear voice of God as He guides you into His perfect will.

Dearest Saint Thérèse, you encountered what seemed to be an immovable obstacle toward the fulfillment of God's will in your life. Pray for me, that when I meet with similar challenges, I will see them as opportunities to grow stronger in my resolve to answer God's call in my life. May I never be deterred from saying "Yes" to the perfect will of God in all things. Saint Thérèse, pray for us.

Lesson Forty-Six — Raptures of Love

Lesson: In many ways, Thérèse was an ordinary teenage girl, and in many other ways she was exceptionally unique. Though her intelligence and virtue helped her stand out, it was her deep love of God which was her most beautiful quality.

> To all appearances my life seemed to continue as formerly. I went on studying, and, what is more important, I went on growing in the love of God. Now and then I experienced what were indeed raptures of love.

Not many teenage girls experience "raptures of love" that are directed toward God. While most girls her age were mesmerized by boys and concerned about their own physical appearance, Thérèse was mesmerized by God. She continually pondered ways in which she could show Him how much she loved Him.

One day Thérèse had the sorrowful thought that God was not loved in Hell. This thought caused her much grief, primarily because Thérèse wanted God to receive love from everywhere. After pondering this, she cried out from the depths of her heart, "I would gladly be cast into that place of torment and blasphemy so that He might be eternally loved even there." Of course she realized that going to Hell would not honor God, but she did not fear Hell because she was certain that "nothing could separate me from the Divine Being Who held me captive." Thérèse was truly held captive by the love of God, and she knew that there was nothing that could ever separate her from Him.

Reflection: What is it in life that most captures your attention, consumes your desires and fills you with a deep longing? Is it love? If it is true love, then this love will be centered in God, will flow from His heart and will be sustained by His grace. How often do you find yourself pondering ways by which you can more fully express your love to God? Do you ever find yourself thinking this way? If the answer is "No," ask yourself the question, "Why?" When God captivates a soul, that soul will want to love Him and receive His love in return.

Ponder the love of God this day and ponder the way Thérèse loved God. Pray that the love that was alive in her heart will also consume your heart and that God will be honored, loved and adored in your life and in the lives of all.

Dearest Saint Thérèse, your heart was on fire for the love of God. This love consumed you and filled you with the sweetest delight. Pray for me, that I may also come to know the love of God to such a degree that I long to love Him as my greatest and all-consuming desire. May my love of God be at the center of my life and direct every action I perform. Saint Thérèse, pray for us.

Lesson Forty-Seven — A "Wondrous Peace" in the Face of Opposition

Lesson: On October 31, 1887, fourteen-year-old Thérèse put her hair up for the first time in an attempt to look older and journeyed with her father to meet the Bishop of Bayeux to gain his permission to enter Carmel at the age of fifteen. Though the Bishop was very cordial and fatherly toward Thérèse, he had to inform her that he could not give his permission until he spoke to Canon Delatroette, the Ecclesiastical Superior of the Lisieux Carmel. Chances did not look promising for Thérèse to enter Carmel early. It was unheard of for a fifteen-year-old girl to make such a radical decision, and the fierce opposition of Canon Delatroette only made the situation more complicated.

> We had to return to Lisieux without a favourable answer. It seemed to me as though my future was shattered forever; the nearer I drew to the goal, the greater my difficulties became. But all the time I felt deep down in my heart a wondrous peace, because I knew that I was only seeking the Will of my Lord.

How wonderful it is to have a "wondrous peace" in the face of opposition. In this case, it was the Bishop and the Ecclesiastical Superior who were the obstacle to Thérèse answering her call. But her peace was present because she only wanted the will of God—nothing more, nothing less, nothing other.

At times, in our zeal for goodness and in our desire to serve God's will, we can become overly zealous and end up pushing things faster than God is leading them. Thérèse teaches the beautiful lesson that nothing can steal away our peace when we are seeking only God's will and not our own. When we are pursuing God's will, no barrier other than ourselves can keep us from fulfilling it.

Reflection: Are you zealous for the will of God in your life? Is there anything God has called you to do that seems difficult to fulfill? If so, put your eyes on His will and seek nothing but that which He wills.

It is easy to get discouraged when we encounter obstacles that appear to inhibit us from doing great good for God and the Church. But God often allows those obstacles for a time to test our resolve and to strengthen our faith. Reflect upon the ways that God has tested you in life and pray for peace as you seek to endure each and every trial.

Dearest Saint Thérèse, you were at peace in the midst of the most difficult obstacles you faced as you sought to answer God's call to live out your vocation of love. Pray for me, that I may always know the will of God and respond to it with complete resolve, trusting in His guiding hand. Saint Thérèse, pray for us.

Chapter Six

Pilgrimage to Rome

Lesson Forty-Eight — Preserving the "Salt of the Earth"

Lesson: Three days after meeting with the Bishop of Bayeux, Thérèse and Céline joined their father on a pilgrimage to the holy city of Rome. All the monuments, buildings and works of art were stunning, but they also taught her of the vanity of this passing world. What touched her the most was the knowledge that she was walking in the footsteps of so many saints of old, especially the Apostles and the Martyrs.

Thérèse and Céline found themselves surrounded by many distinguished people whose fancy titles seemed to be nothing more than a "vapor of smoke." She pondered these titles and earthly status and realized that those who are the poorest and the least-known on Earth, for love of God, "will be the first, the noblest, and the richest" in Heaven.

Thérèse also discovered one new and very important aspect of her future vocation. Up until that time, she always presumed that the soul of every priest was "as pure as crystal." During the pilgrimage, she encountered many priests and began to realize that "even though the sublime dignity of Priesthood raises them higher than the Angels, they are still but weak and imperfect men." This, however, did not discourage her. Instead, it gave her a new understanding of her future vocation as a Carmelite to pray and sacrifice for priests. She rejoiced to think that it was her mission to "preserve the salt of the Earth" in the soul of every priest.

> We offer our prayers and sacrifices for the apostles of the Lord; we ourselves ought to be their apostles, while they, by word and example, are preaching the Gospel to our brethren. Have we not a glorious mission to fulfill?

Reflection: When you look at the diversity of people all around you, you will discover that some are very visible and honored by society, while others are silent and hidden. Some are given a dignity above the angels, while others seem to be stripped even of their human dignity. Some are wealthy and some are poor. Some are great sinners; some are living saints.

In the eyes of God, all that matters is that we are faithful to the particular mission He gives us. If that means God wants you to receive many worldly honors, so be it. If that means you are to live a hidden and humble life, so be it. If that means you are to be a priest, so be it. And if that means you are to be a cloistered nun who prays for priests and other sinners, so be it.

Reflect upon those whom you may envy in life. As you do, instead of envying them, pray for them. Offer sacrifices for them and beg God to keep them faithful to the vocation they have received. As Thérèse discovered her call to pray for priests, so you may discover your call to pray for others who are in need. Reflect also upon the great reward awaiting us all in Heaven if we are but faithful here on Earth. Earthly honors will mean nothing in Heaven. The virtues of faith, hope and charity will be the only marks of distinction that will remain with us forever.

Saint Thérèse, your simple and humble eyes could see beyond the superficial "dignities" of this world. You also were able to see the dignity of priests, despite their many sins. Pray for me, that I may see all people as God sees them. May I love each person, rejoice in each one's unique vocation and pray for all that they may grow in the eternal virtues. Saint Thérèse, pray for us.

Lesson Forty-Nine — Childlike Conversation with the Mother of God

Lesson: On route to Rome, Thérèse's pilgrimage stopped in Paris, and she was blessed to visit the Shrine of Our Lady of Victories! What a joy and blessing this was.

> In this holy spot the Blessed Virgin, my Mother, told me plainly that it was really she who had smiled on me and cured me. With intense fervour I entreated her to keep me always, and to realise my heart's desire by hiding me under her spotless mantle, and I also asked her to remove from me every occasion of sin.

Thérèse recounts that the "Blessed Virgin, my Mother, told me plainly…" This statement reveals Thérèse's intimate connection to the Mother of God. Our Lady most likely did not appear to Thérèse in a physical form. Nonetheless, the Blessed Mother did speak "plainly" to Thérèse. This was only possible because Thérèse was so in tune with the voice of God and her heavenly Mother. The innocence, certitude and clarity with which she spoke about this conversation with the Mother of God is itself a testimony to how completely Thérèse was walking in faith.

She also spoke her prayer to her Mother as a child would speak. She asked to be held close to her and not only to remove every sin, but even every "occasion of sin." Thérèse's prayer was answered because she asked with the simplicity of a pure faith.

Reflection: When you speak to God or to our Blessed Mother, how do you pray? Do you speak with the utmost confidence and with the clearest conviction? Do you ask only for those good things that make up the will of God, or do you seek to impose your own will upon God and our Blessed Mother by making selfish requests that do not conform to the will of God?

When God or our Blessed Mother speaks to you, do you hear? So often we do not hear a heavenly voice because we do not know how to listen. Thérèse knew how to listen, and so she heard Our Lady as clearly as she heard her sisters or her father speak to her.

Seek to imitate this childlike conversation of Thérèse so that the love you share with the Mother of God will be as real as real can be.

Saint Thérèse, you listened to and spoke to the Mother of God as a loving and attentive daughter would speak to her mother. Pray for me, that I may grow in faith and be attentive to our merciful God, to my Blessed Mother and to all the angels and saints. May I know them, love them and follow their commands every moment of my life. Saint Thérèse, pray for us.

Lesson Fifty — A Glimpse of Heaven

Lesson: On the train from Paris to Rome, Thérèse passed through Switzerland and was deeply impressed by the scenery of the mountains, sky, meadows, lakes, valleys and hills. It was all "so full of poetry and grandeur." As she pondered nature, she realized that this incredible scenery was a "foretaste of the wonders of Heaven." She also realized that once she entered the walls of Carmel, she would never see such beauty on Earth again. But this did not discourage her.

> Later on, when the time of trial comes, when I am enclosed in the Carmel and shall only be able to see a little bit of sky, I will remember this day and it will encourage me. I will make light of my own small interests by thinking of the greatness and majesty of God; I will love Him alone, and will not be so foolish as to attach myself to the fleeting trifles of this world, now that my heart has had a glimpse of what is reserved for those who love Him.

Thérèse realized that she did not need to be continually entertained by the things of the world, or even the beauty of nature. She was given her little glimpse of Heaven on Earth and that was all she needed. She would remember this scene and allow it to continually remind her of what awaits us all in Heaven.

Reflection: Have you had an experience in life through which you received a glimpse of Heaven? Perhaps it was a stunning view of nature, or a moment of deep prayer, an act of profound charity from another, or some other encounter that changed your life. Remember those moments and allow their lessons to be continually imprinted on your soul.

Thérèse took a mental "snapshot" of this little Heaven on Earth in order to save it for the future when she knew she would experience "the time of trial" within the walls of Carmel. Know that trials will come, just as they did for

Thérèse. But do not forget the lessons God has taught you through life, and do not fail to recall those lessons when you need them the most.

Dearest Saint Thérèse, you were given a small glimpse of Heaven as you gazed upon the natural beauty God placed before your eyes. Pray for me, that I may understand the true beauty of Heaven and may be open to the many ways God wants to teach me its lessons. May I always be open to what God teaches and bring those lessons to the trials of life. Saint Thérèse, pray for us.

Lesson Fifty-One — A Prism of Faith

Lesson: As Thérèse and her fellow pilgrims continued to Rome, they made many stops along the way. They saw the cities of Northern Italy and had many new experiences. Though she was intrigued with the beautiful architecture, sculptures, paintings and historical monuments, she was always looking at what she saw through her "prism of faith." For example, while in Venice, she visited the Palace of the Doges and saw the prisons that so many had occupied of old.

> While visiting these dreadful prisons I fancied myself in the times of the martyrs, and gladly would I have chosen this sombre abode for my dwelling if there had been any question of confessing my faith.

Her faith was always on her mind. All of these most magnificent monuments, works of art and historical buildings had to be analyzed by her through the prism of her faith. Some sites and experiences taught her about the vanity of the world. Others helped her renew her willingness to be a martyr. Still others made her think of what awaited her at Carmel. God was always on her mind.

Reflection: How about you? What do you think about all day long? A good way to examine your conscience is by considering what you spend the most time thinking about throughout your day. Is God always on your mind?

Allow this young teenager to teach you about the only "prism" through which you must see the world and your experiences in life. Seek to imitate Thérèse's Little Way and to learn all of life's lessons through this prism of faith.

Dearest Saint Thérèse, as you grew and matured, and as you encountered many new people, places, and experiences in life, you saw all through the prism of faith. Pray for me, that I may see all things with the eyes of faith. May I never be seduced by the enticements of the world, and may I always encounter life with the eyes of God. Saint Thérèse, pray for us.

Lesson Fifty-Two — The Holy House

Lesson: One inspiring place Thérèse visited was the Holy House of Loreto. The Holy House is said to be the actual house of Jesus, Mary and Joseph in Jerusalem. In the year 1294, tradition states that angels miraculously carried the house from Jerusalem to various sites in Italy, until finally being transported to Loreto in 1295. Thérèse was deeply impressed with this house and inspired by the thought of looking at and touching the same walls and floor that housed the Holy Family. She stated, "I was overwhelmed with emotion when I realised that I was under the very roof that had sheltered the Holy Family."

Even this most sacred encounter with the home of the Holy Family drew Thérèse to ponder an even deeper mystery.

> But our greatest joy was to receive Jesus in His own House, and thus become His living temple in the very place which He had honoured by His Divine Presence.

When someone is in love, a mere picture or artifact of the loved one cannot compare with that person's real presence. Though she was inspired by the ancient little house, she was more inspired by being able to touch and consume her Lord in Holy Communion and adore His True Presence in the Tabernacle.

> What will be our joy when we communicate eternally in the dwelling of the King of Heaven? It will be undimmed by the grief of parting, and will know no end. His House will be ours for all eternity

Reflection: What inspires you the most in this world? Is it the Blessed Sacrament? Our Lord, present in the Blessed Sacrament, is the most amazing and awe-inspiring mystery this world has ever known. For Jesus to come to us in this form and to humbly manifest His very Heart and Soul under the appearance of bread and wine is the true Miracle of all miracles.

Reflect upon how deeply you love our Lord in this precious gift. Seek to imitate the great faith and devotion of this teenage girl. Thérèse's greatest joy was to be with our Lord in the Blessed Sacrament. Pray that this same joy floods your heart.

Dearest Saint Thérèse, you discovered the great joy of receiving our Lord in the Blessed Sacrament and longed for Him every time He was near, hidden as a Prisoner of Love in the Tabernacle. Pray for me, that I may also burn with a deep desire to receive our Lord in the Most Holy Eucharist. May I become His new temple and a tabernacle for His Holy Presence. Saint Thérèse, pray for us.

Lesson Fifty-Three — The Greatest Wonder in Rome

Lesson: Thérèse spent six days visiting all the many wonderful sites of Rome. She saw the Coliseum where the blood of many martyrs was shed. She visited the Catacombs and lay in the very resting place of the little martyr Saint Cecilia. She went to the church of Saint Agnes and thought about her sister Pauline, now Sister Agnes of Jesus who was back in Carmel. After visiting many other holy sites, it was on her seventh day in Rome that Thérèse saw the greatest wonder Rome had to offer...the Holy Father himself!

On Sunday morning, November 20, Thérèse and the other pilgrims were blessed to attend Mass with Pope Leo XIII in his private chapel. Afterwards, each pilgrim was invited to come kneel before the Holy Father to receive his blessing in silence. The Vicar-General of Bayeux, Father Révérony, had made it clear to everyone that they were not to speak to the Holy Father. When Thérèse heard this, she turned to

Céline to inquire from her what she should do. Céline quietly told her, "Speak!" Sure enough, when it was Thérèse's turn she knelt and, with tears of hope in her eyes, made her sweet request of the Holy Father that he permit her to enter Carmel at the age of fifteen. The Holy Father listened to her and eventually responded in a thoughtful way, "Well, my child, do whatever the Superiors decide." Thérèse made one more attempt and the Holy Father responded by saying, "Well, well! You will enter if it is God's Will." With that, Thérèse had to rise and exit without the immediate permission she sought.

In pondering this later, Thérèse realized that the Holy Father spoke in a prophetic way. She did end up entering at age fifteen because it *was* the will of God. God's will cannot be stopped when we cooperate with it. Not even those who have much authority, even within the Church, can thwart the will of God when the faithful are obedient to His gentle promptings of grace.

Reflection: How far are you willing to go to fulfill the will of God in your life? Sometimes God allows what appears to be insurmountable obstacles to arise in our lives so that He can strengthen us and test our resolve.

Reflect upon your own response to obstacles that seem insurmountable. Nothing is impossible for God when He wills it. Our one and only duty is to be obedient to Him in all things. When we are obedient and do not waver, God will move mountains and provide clear passage for the fulfillment of His perfect plan.

Dearest Saint Thérèse, you faced one obstacle after another as you sought to answer God's call to enter Carmel at the age of fifteen. In the face of every challenge, you responded with faith and hope. Pray for me, that I may also live in faith and in hope throughout my life, to say "Yes" to God's perfect will, no matter the cost and no matter how hard. May I imitate your determination of faith and continue down the glorious path God has prepared for my life. Saint Thérèse, pray for us.

Lesson Fifty-Four — The Only Joy of the Soul

Lesson: As Thérèse and her fellow pilgrims continued to journey through various towns of Italy, they daily stayed in some of the nicest hotels. But these "splendid" hotels lent themselves to more reflection by Thérèse.

> I realised thoroughly that joy is not found in the things which surround us, but lives only in the soul. One could possess it as well in an obscure prison as in the palace of a king. And so now I am happier at the Carmel, in the midst of trials within and without, than I was in the world where I had everything I wanted, and, above all, the joys of a happy home.

Thérèse was staying in the best hotels, and back in Lisieux she was blessed with such a happy home. Though she was grateful for these earthly blessings, she was also keenly aware that none of them could give her true joy. Joy was found "only in the soul." And no matter if she were in the most luxurious surroundings or in the darkest prison, joy in the soul had its origin only in God and in the fulfillment of

His perfect will. For her, that fulfillment would be achieved only in Carmel.

Reflection: Do you have true joy in your life? Sometimes you might be deceived by passing pleasures in life, equating them with joy. But joy is a spiritual gift that comes only from God and that lives within the depths of your soul. Have you encountered this spiritual gift from God?

Reflect upon the difference between "pleasure" and "joy." The things of this world offer pleasure, but they do not offer joy. Seek to be obedient to the will of God. In that single-minded commitment, you will find the joy that your soul seeks.

Dearest Saint Thérèse, as you journeyed through the beautiful and impressive towns of Italy, your heart's desire was set upon the hidden walls of Carmel where you knew you would find the joy you sought. Pray for me, that I may keep my eyes fixed upon the one joy of fulfilling the will of God in my life. May I, like you, never be deterred or seduced by the passing pleasures of this world and seek only that which is eternal. Saint Thérèse, pray for us.

Lesson Fifty-Five — God Alone

Lesson: Clearly, Thérèse had just one thing on her mind throughout her pilgrimage. No matter what she saw and no matter whom she encountered, she kept focused upon the call God was placing in her heart. By this time, she had exhausted every earthly means of achieving the will of God to enter Carmel at age fifteen. She had spoken to the Mother of Carmel, the priest Superior, the Vicar General, the Bishop and even the Pope. Though she had not yet obtained the "Yes" she sought, she did not give up.

After visiting Assisi, where Saint Francis and Saint Clare lived their inspiring lives, she ended up in the last carriage to leave, which was the carriage of the Vicar General, Father Révérony. He was very kind to her and from time to time spoke to her about Carmel, promising that he would do everything possible to help her enter at age fifteen.

> This meeting was like balm to my wounds, though it did not prevent me from suffering. I had now lost all trust in creatures and could only lean on God Himself.

Though Thérèse was consoled by the promise of this good priest to help her enter Carmel, she had learned a valuable lesson. In the end, God alone was worthy of her complete trust. Human beings will always fail in one way or another. Even those within the Church will, at times, hinder the will of God. But that was no reason to lose trust. Instead, Thérèse resolved to trust more deeply and to trust in God alone.

Reflection: We have all met with the sins and weaknesses of others. This can be the cause of discouragement, but it can also become the source of deeper trust in God alone.

Do you have a difficult time trusting? Is there someone in your life who has tempted you to lose trust and turn toward discouragement? If so, reflect upon this temptation and allow it to become the source of your deeper trust in God. God can and will do all good things in our lives when we trust that He can work miracles, despite the weaknesses and sins of those all around us, including ourselves.

Dearest Saint Thérèse, your determination and devotion to answering your call are inspiring. Pray for me, that I will not allow anything to hinder me from seeking and fulfilling the will of God in my life. May I trust in all things and allow my trust to be centered in God alone. Saint Thérèse, pray for us.

Lesson Fifty-Six — Perseverance Transformed

Lesson: After Thérèse returned from her pilgrimage, she went to Carmel to share her thoughts and experiences with Mother Marie de Gonzague who instructed her to write to the Bishop to remind him of his promise. Thérèse did this immediately. She wrote a number of drafts, but before the letter was sent, both Pauline and Mother Marie de Gonzague had second thoughts about the wisdom of writing the Bishop. However, her letter was finally sent in hopes that Thérèse would receive a favorable response before Christmas. Every day she and her father went to the post office to look for her letter of permission, but it never arrived. Finally, she had to accept that she would not enter before Christmas.

On December 28, Mother Marie received a letter from the Bishop granting his permission, and it was with great joy, mixed with sorrow, that Thérèse received word of this on January 1. God had worked His miracle! Pauline, however, now wanted Thérèse to wait until <u>after</u> Easter to enter!

Their father was upset about this, but Thérèse accepted this decision with much grace.

> I could not restrain my tears at the thought of such a long delay. This trial affected me in a special manner, for I felt my earthly ties were severed, and yet the Ark in its turn refused to admit the poor little dove.

The plans and correspondence continued, and Thérèse experienced many emotions. This lovely girl of fifteen had persevered and was now able to formally take up her Carmelite cross on April 9, 1888, at the age of fifteen.

Reflection: Perseverance is difficult to endure while we are actually in the act of persevering. Yet when we see that the fruits of our efforts are rewarded by the fulfillment of God's will, all the suffering that was endured is turned sweet and becomes our reward.

Is there something in your life at this moment through which God wants you to persevere? Is there some trial that is painful, confusing and difficult to endure? If so, press on. Do not be deterred by the difficulty. Instead, look forward to reaping the reward of your fidelity. God is always faithful, and He will repay your perseverance a hundredfold.

Dearest Saint Thérèse, you never despaired down the path toward your vocation, even though it was a path difficult to travel. Pray for me, that I may persevere through my own trials in life and do so with strength and confidence. May I imitate you and also be rewarded for my fidelity to the will of God. Saint Thérèse, pray for us.

Chapter Seven

The Little Flower Enters the Carmel

Lesson Fifty-Seven — The Wound of Love... Once Again

Lesson: Recall the "wound of love" that Thérèse experienced at the loss of her mother (Lesson Fifteen). She loved her mother so deeply that her passing left a wound which only slowly healed with the help of the tender love and care she received from her father and sisters.

Just over a decade later, the evening before she entered her beloved Carmel, she felt that wound of love once again. She was at table with her father and her sisters Céline and Léonie for the last time in their family home.

> These farewells are in themselves heartrending, and just when I would have liked to be forgotten I received the tenderest expressions of affection, as if to increase the pain of parting.

The next morning, April 9, 1888, Thérèse and her family attended the early Mass at Carmel. After Communion, Thérèse "heard sobs on all sides." After Mass, she and her family members exchanged their final acts of love.

> As I led the way to the cloister door my heart beat so violently that I wondered if I were going to die. Oh, the agony of that moment! One must have experienced it in order to understand. I embraced all my dear ones and knelt for my Father's blessing. He, too, knelt down and blessed me through his tears. It was a sight to gladden the Angels, this old man giving his child to God while she was yet in the springtime of life.

"A sight to gladden the Angels," yet this parting inflicted a deep wound of love. They felt this beautiful moment so deeply because the Martin family shared a bond that was pure, holy and selfless. God was asking for the greatest sacrifice from them, and they all responded with submission and love. Love is "painful" in the sense that, when it is pure and holy, it is also sacrificial, selfless and self-giving. Sacrifice "wounds" us with a holy wound that is also sweet and healing. This wound of love is best depicted by the Sacred Heart of Jesus, wounded on the Cross and resulting in the outpouring of His endless mercy.

Reflection: Whom do you love so deeply that it hurts? Does your heart ache for the goodness of another and love that person such that you are willing to love sacrificially, offering your beloved to the divine will—no matter what it may be?

We all love in various ways and on various levels. Reflect upon the way you give and receive love in the relationships in your life. Reflect upon this father offering his daughter to God and upon this daughter lovingly enduring her father's and sisters' pain in giving her to God. This is indeed a love which gladdens the Angels and a love which we must all seek to imitate in our lives.

Dearest Saint Thérèse, you were exceptionally blessed to give and receive a love that was so deep and pure that it left a sacrificial wound of love. Pray for me, that I may imitate this depth of love. May I also gladden the Angels by the sacrifice and offering I make in the fulfillment of God's perfect will. Saint Thérèse, pray for us.

Lesson Fifty-Eight — Peace Amidst Every Trial

Lesson: Recall the "wondrous peace" that Thérèse felt, even as she endured many obstacles in her attempt to fulfill God's will and enter Carmel at the age of fifteen (See Lesson Forty-Seven). As a young teenager, Thérèse of the Child Jesus continued to receive peace as she began her new cloistered life in the convent.

At last my desires were realised, and I cannot describe the deep sweet peace which filled my soul. This peace has remained with me during the eight and a half years of my life here, and has never left me even amid the greatest trials.

It's important to note that, in the experience of Sister Thérèse, deep peace did not exclude "the greatest trials" she would endure during her years as a Carmelite nun. Peace, joy, faith, fortitude and the like do not eliminate trials from our lives, rather, they have the effect of transforming trials into the path to holiness.

Everything in the Convent delighted me, especially our little cell. I fancied myself transported to the desert. I repeat that my happiness was calm and peaceful—not even the lightest breeze ruffled the tranquil waters on which my little barque sailed; no cloud darkened the blue sky. I felt fully recompensed for all I had gone through, and I kept saying: "Now I am here forever." ...Yet you know well that from the beginning my way was strewn with thorns rather than with roses.

Reflection: What trials have you experienced in life? If you are going through some trial right now, do not lose hope and do not lose your peace. Pain and suffering are a part of life. The good news we must never forget is that Jesus transformed suffering, and as a result, made it possible for every trial we would endure to become the means of our sanctity.

Reflect upon your experience of your own trials, and if you see that they have stolen away your peace, get on your knees and surrender your heart more deeply to God. He desires to be with you through all things and will carry you when you need it the most.

Dearest Saint Thérèse, you were blessed with the most wondrous peace throughout your life on account of your deep trust in God. Pray for me, that I may persevere through all things and may always live in the peace that comes with the fulfillment of the will of God. May your example inspire me and lead me to holiness. Saint Thérèse, pray for us.

Lesson Fifty-Nine — An Inestimable Grace

Lesson: The new postulant, Thérèse of the Child Jesus, embraced her new life as a Carmelite with fervor and joy. Her daily schedule included six hours of prayer, a half hour of spiritual reading, five hours of work, seven hours for sleep, two meals in silence with the community while some text was read aloud, two hours of recreation with the other sisters and an hour of free time.

Thérèse received two incredible graces once she entered Carmel. First, she received the gift of spiritual dryness which was a lack of spiritual consolation and a feeling as if God were absent. Second, she received the gift of severe mistreatment at the hands of the Mother Superior, Mother Marie de Gonzague. Most people would not consider these two "gifts" as "inestimable graces," but Thérèse of the

Child Jesus was able to see beyond the surface and discover the rich spiritual blessings she received from them.

> In the first place, my soul had for its daily food the bread of spiritual dryness. Then, too, dear Mother, Our Lord allowed you, unconsciously, to treat me very severely. You found fault with me whenever you met me. I remember once I had left a cobweb in the cloister, and you said to me before the whole community: "It is easy to see that our cloisters are swept by a child of fifteen. It is disgraceful! Go and sweep away that cobweb, and be more careful in future."

> ...And yet, dear Mother, how grateful I am to you for giving me such a sound and valuable training. It was an inestimable grace. What should I have become, if, as the world outside believed, I had been but the pet of the Community?

> ...Suffering opened her arms to me from the first, and I took her to my heart.

> ...For five years this way was mine, but I alone knew it; this was precisely the flower I wished to offer to Jesus, a hidden flower which keeps its perfume only for Heaven.

Thérèse could see that the suffering she endured was producing much fruit in her soul and was becoming a precious "perfume" for Heaven. Her spiritual director also saw her soul grow in holiness, for she recalled, "Two months after my entry Father Pichon was surprised at the workings of grace in my soul; he thought my piety childlike and my path an easy one." God was indeed doing great things in His Little Flower.

Reflection: Whether you experience spiritual dryness, severe treatment from another, or some other suffering in your life, it is difficult to see the blessing that comes from such experiences. Thérèse of the Child Jesus was different. She was not self-consumed and did not pity her mistreatment or her interior cross. She kept her eyes only on the sweet fragrance that God was bringing forth from her soul for Him alone to enjoy. This knowledge enabled her to keep her peace and joy through every daily cross.

Reflect upon your own attitude toward the sufferings you endure. Pray that you will receive the "inestimable grace" to see beyond the superficial pain that is inflicted and will be able to allow the healing balm of grace to transform everything in your life into a beautiful fragrance for God.

Saint Thérèse, your attitude toward the suffering you endured, both interiorly and exteriorly, is inspiring and is a reflection of your deep union with Jesus on the Cross. Pray for me, that I may imitate your complete embrace of every suffering in my life so as to become a sweet fragrance of love offered to our merciful God. Saint Thérèse, pray for us.

Lesson Sixty — A Simple Soul

Lesson: Shortly after Thérèse of the Child Jesus entered Carmel, Father Pichon, a saintly priest, was appointed as her Spiritual Director. After making a general confession of her whole life, Father Pichon declared, "Before God, the

Blessed Virgin, and Angels, and all the Saints, I declare that you have never committed a mortal sin."

Thérèse tried hard to share every aspect of her soul each time she met with Father Pichon but found it difficult to know what to say. The same was true with her Novice Mistress (Pauline), even though she found her to be exceedingly good to her. One day during recreation, one of the older sisters mentioned to Thérèse that she understood that Thérèse did not know what to say in spiritual direction and with her superiors. Thérèse was surprised at this and asked her how she knew.

> "Because your soul is very simple; but when you are perfect you will become more simple still. The nearer one approaches God, the simpler one becomes."

> This good Mother was right. Nevertheless the great difficulty I found in opening my heart, though it came from simplicity, was a genuine trial. Now, however, without having lost my simplicity, I am able to express my thoughts with the greatest ease.

Thérèse was, indeed, a simple soul. She was simple because even though God is the deepest and widest Mystery, God is also exceedingly simple. God is love, simple and pure. Thérèse was in love with her God and the deeper her love grew, the simpler she became.

Reflection: For us, life can seem extraordinarily complicated and complex, but it doesn't have to be. We must all seek to become more simple as we grow in love of God and in virtue. The greater the love in our soul, the simpler our lives become. With simplicity, our lives are then freed from the many burdens and complexities that weigh us down.

Do you find yourself weighed down at times by the complexities of life? If so, ponder the simplicity of love. If love of God and others is your single focus in life, many of the difficulties, confusions and burdens you carry will begin to disappear.

Saint Thérèse, you were a simple soul who was free from the many burdens and complexities of life. Pray for me, that I may seek the simplicity of life that you enjoyed and that I will find the freedom that comes from the simple love of God and others. Saint Thérèse, pray for us.

Lesson Sixty-One — The Holy Face of Jesus

Lesson: Thérèse of the Child Jesus had always adored the Holy Face of Jesus imprinted on the veil of Saint Veronica when she lovingly wiped His face on the road to Calvary. Thérèse's devotion to the Holy Face further increased with imparted wisdom from her sister, Sister Agnes of Jesus, as well as from Mother Marie de Gonzague.

This devotion inspired Thérèse in two ways. First, she sought to be like Saint Veronica, offering consolation to her suffering Lord through her tender love and devotion. Second, she sought to become the Face of Jesus.

> I wished that my face, like the Face of Jesus, "should be, as it were, hidden and despised" (Is.

53:3), so that no one on earth should esteem me. I thirsted to suffer and to be forgotten.

Thérèse pondered the great mystery, that the bruised and beaten Face of Jesus was but a veil for the Holy Face of God. God was hidden and His face despised by many. Only by faith could one see behind the veil to the reality of His glory.

Thérèse discovered that this was also her mission. One aspect of her imitation of our Lord was to live her life hidden and despised on the surface by the world, but holy and united to God in the depths of her soul.

Thérèse's love for the Holy Face was so important to her that she obtained permission, when she made her profession as a novice, to change her name to Thérèse of the Child Jesus and the Holy Face.

PRAYER TO THE HOLY FACE

O Adorable Face of Jesus, sole beauty which ravisheth my heart, vouchsafe to impress on my soul Thy Divine Likeness, so that it may not be possible for Thee to look at Thy Spouse without beholding Thyself. O my Beloved, for love of Thee I am content not to see here on earth the sweetness of Thy Glance, nor to feel the ineffable Kiss of Thy Sacred Lips, but I beg of Thee to inflame me with Thy Love, so that it may consume me quickly, and that soon *Teresa of the Holy Face* may behold Thy glorious Countenance in Heaven.

Reflection: What devotion or inspiration has affected you so deeply that you long to identify yourself with it throughout your life? Thérèse discovered her vocation of hiddenness in the devotion to the Holy Face. You too must seek your vocation in the devotion that God has uniquely called you to embrace.

Reflect upon the Scriptures, teachings or devotions in your life that have had the greatest impact upon you. As you do, allow them to guide you in the vocation that God has given to you.

Saint Thérèse, you discovered a central aspect of your unique vocation in the Holy Face of Jesus. Pray for me, that I may also discover my vocation through the ways that God has spoken to me and inspired me along the way. May I embrace His holy words and inspiration and allow them to transform me into the person I am called to become. Saint Thérèse, pray for us.

Lesson Sixty-Two — An Offering and a Victim

Lesson: Thérèse recalled a moment from her childhood when her father spoke to her and her sisters about his desire to become a victim for God.

> "Children, I have just come back from Alençon, and there, in the Church of Notre Dame, I received such graces and consolations that I made this prayer: 'My God, it is too much, yes, I am too happy; I shall not get to Heaven like this, I wish to suffer something for Thee—and I offered myself as a'"—the word *victim* died on his lips.

Mr. Martin was indeed a victim. One by one God called His daughters to Himself, and one by one Mr. Martin generously offered his daughters to God. The sacrifice was deep but also filled him with great joy. His suffering increased in his old age, but the greatest source of his victimhood was his complete generosity with God, giving Him the very best he had...his beloved children.

After Thérèse had entered Carmel, Céline confided in her father that she wished to follow her sisters. Instead of feeling sorrow at Céline's announcement, Mr. Martin was filled with joy.

> "Let us go before the Blessed Sacrament," he said, "and thank God for all the graces He has granted us and the honour He has paid me in choosing His Spouses from my household. God has indeed done me great honour in asking for my children. If I possessed anything better I would hasten to offer it to Him."

Mr. Martin did have more to give. Thérèse noted that, "That something better was himself..." Saint Louis Martin not only joyfully offered every daughter he had to God, but at the end of his life offered himself to God to experience great physical suffering. His life was a holocaust of love because he was not only the one making a generous offering to God, he was also the one who was offered. He was a holy victim of love.

Reflection: Sacrifice is difficult. Oftentimes we only want to give a little to God. But God wants not only the best we have to offer, He wants *everything* we have to offer. Just as

Jesus gave His life to the last drop of blood, so we must make our lives a sacrifice of perfect love. We must sacrifice all to God, ultimately making ourselves the *victim* of love that is offered.

How generous are you with your life? Do you hold the best part back for yourself? Or do you give everything? Be generous with God to the end, and God's generosity toward you will be repaid beyond measure.

Saint Louis Martin, father of Saint Thérèse, you were most generous in your love of God. You gave not only your daughters as a total sacrifice to God, you also gave your very life. Pray for me, that I may imitate your generosity and hold nothing back as my offering, entrusting all to our merciful God. Saint Louis and Saint Thérèse, pray for us.

Lesson Sixty-Three — A Bitter Chalice of Interior Suffering

Lesson: In June of 1888, two months after Thérèse had entered the walls of Carmel, she said to her Novice Mistress (Sister Agnes of Jesus), "I am suffering a great deal, Mother, yet I feel I can suffer still more." As she spoke those words, Thérèse of the Child Jesus did not understand the suffering she was about to endure.

It was especially on her four-day retreat, just prior to receiving her habit on January 10, 1889, that Thérèse began to drink from her "bitter chalice." She wrote several letters during this retreat to her sister, Sister Agnes of Jesus.

[Jesus] is riddling me with *pinpricks;* the poor little ball is exhausted. All over it has very little holes which make it suffer more than if it had only one large one!...Nothing near Jesus. Aridity!...Sleep!...

Today more than yesterday, if it were possible, I was deprived of all consolation. I thank Jesus, who finds this good for my soul, and that, perhaps if He were to console me, I would stop at this sweetness; but He wants that *all* be for *Himself!*...Well, then, *all* will be for Him, all, even when I feel I am able to offer nothing; so, just like this evening, I will give Him this nothing!

In one short letter to Sister Agnes, Thérèse used 23 exclamation points, revealing the intensity of her interior suffering. She had no consolation, only interior agony. In another letter to Sister Agnes, she stated, "Oh! If it were not you I would not dare send these thoughts, the most intimate of *my soul!*...**I beg you,** tear up these sheets after you have read them!" She concluded, "Pray for your little daughter that she may refuse Jesus not one *atom* of her heart."

Through every interior suffering Thérèse endured, she never lost her peace. This peace enabled her to deepen her love for Jesus and to offer Him the "nothing" that she felt. She did not love Him because He consoled her; she loved Him simply because He was worthy of <u>all</u> love. And in the gift of all her love, she continued to grow into the most pure and holy spouse of her Beloved, becoming transformed every day into "the happiest of mortals."

Reflection: God's love, as it is lavished upon the saints, is mysterious. For many, the interior suffering He inflicts upon a pure and holy soul does not make sense. But for the saint, these wounds of love inflicted by the Beloved Himself have one central and defining characteristic: They strengthen love.

Have you felt some affliction in your life? Perhaps it was interior or perhaps it was something imposed upon you from outside. When you suffer, how do you respond? Many will turn to self-pity or some other form of selfish consolation to remove the pain. But if you are willing to enter into the mystery of God's love, allow yourself to see every affliction you experience as an invitation to choose Jesus on a deeper level for the sake of love alone. When love feels good, it is easy. When love hurts, it produces holiness. Seek to give God the "nothing" you might feel at times so that even the pain will become sweet and transforming.

Dearest Saint Thérèse, it is impossible to understand what your soul endured due to your burning love of God. Pray for me, that I may understand the mystery of my own suffering and that I may allow it to form my heart into a heart of pure love. May I imitate your selfless "Yes" to God when it is most difficult to do so. Saint Thérèse, pray for us.

Lesson Sixty-Four — "The Little Miracle"

Lesson: January 10, 1889 was set by the Bishop of Bayeux as the clothing day for Thérèse of the Child Jesus.

> Do you remember my telling you, dear Mother, how fond I am of snow? While I was still quite small, its whiteness entranced me. Why had I such a fancy for snow? Perhaps it was because, being a little winter flower, my eyes first saw the earth clad in its beautiful white mantle. So, on my clothing day, I wished to see it decked, like myself, in spotless white.

Unfortunately, the weather was quite mild, and that morning she abandoned her "childish desire" that it would snow.

Her father and sisters arrived to join Thérèse for the ceremony. It was a beautiful celebration, and the Bishop was most kind. He spoke of Thérèse's visit to Bayeux and of her perseverance. The Bishop even told the story of Thérèse putting up her hair for the first time to look older when she came to see him less than two years prior.

At the end of the ceremony, as Thérèse of the Child Jesus and the Holy Face returned to the cloister, she noticed to her surprise that, despite the mild weather, part of the courtyard was actually covered with snow!

> What a delicate attention on the part of Jesus! Gratifying the least wish of His little Spouse, He even sent her this. Where is the creature so mighty that he can make one flake of it fall to please his beloved?

Though Thérèse was willing to go without this little gift, her Jesus offered her this little miracle of love. When two love each other with such a profound love, even the smallest details are never lost. Her Beloved had chosen to offer her this small act of love.

Reflection: How attentive are you to the details of love? We often desire that others be attentive to the details of our lives. When those details are attended to, they can have the effect of making a tremendous difference. And though we tend to desire that others be attentive to the details of our lives, we often fail to be attentive to the details of their lives.

Reflect upon how fully you imitate this small miracle of love shown by Jesus to Thérèse. Allow this act of generosity and perfect thoughtfulness on His part to be a source of inspiration for you in all the relationships you have.

Saint Thérèse, you were blessed with a Spouse whose love and care for you was perfect. Though you did not need this "little miracle," you received it as God's tender gift. Pray for me, that I may turn my eyes to the smallest details of love in others' lives, and through those acts, express the Heart and tenderness of God. Saint Thérèse, pray for us.

Lesson Sixty-Five — The Wedding Preparation

Lesson: Thérèse of the Child Jesus and of the Holy Face now wore the Carmelite clothing of a novice. As she entered into the period of the novitiate, she hoped to make her perpetual vows in one year's time, at the age of seventeen. Once again, God had other plans.

Canon Delatroette, the Carmelite Superior, once again interfered and believed it was better for Thérèse to wait, rather than make her vows right when she turned seventeen.

Though this was difficult to accept, Thérèse did so by looking at the extended period of the novitiate as an opportunity to rid herself of all selfishness and her own will.

> "I do not ask Thee to hasten the day of my profession, I will wait as long as Thou pleasest, only I cannot bear that through any fault of mine my union with Thee should be delayed; I will set to work and carefully prepare a wedding-dress enriched with diamonds and precious stones, and, when Thou findest it sufficiently rich, I am sure that nothing will keep Thee from accepting me as Thy Spouse."

Thérèse knew she should not hasten her "wedding" with her Beloved. She wanted to become His spouse in His timing, and she committed herself to the preparation. As most brides prepare the wedding dress to be beautiful, Thérèse knew that she must prepare her soul as the beautiful garment for her Spouse. If she adorned it with every virtue and precious act of love, her Beloved could never refuse her.

Reflection: What is it in your life that is worth waiting for? Is there something that God is asking you to prepare for with diligence? Too often in life, we can get into the habit of preparing in a sloppy way for those things that should be most important.

Reflect upon those who are most important to you, especially family. Do you give them the best of yourself and your efforts, realizing that no sacrifice or act of love is too great?

Thérèse held nothing back in her preparation for the wedding with her Lord. Seek to imitate her single-minded devotion of love and hold nothing back from the acts of love you are called to offer in life.

Saint Thérèse, you saw the great value of patient preparation for the total gift of yourself to your Beloved Spouse. Pray for me, that I may also be diligent in my acts of love and may count no sacrifice too small or great. May I imitate your patience and dedication to those whom I am to love with my whole soul. Saint Thérèse, pray for us.

Lesson Sixty-Six — Small Hidden Acts of Love

Lesson: During the twenty months that Thérèse of the Child Jesus and the Holy Face prepared for her vows as a novice, she discovered the great power of small hidden acts of love: "Above all I endeavoured to practise little hidden acts of virtue." Through the conscious choice to offer these small and hidden acts, Thérèse did indeed grow in much virtue.

On one occasion a sister accidentally took Thérèse's oil lamp in the evening, leaving Thérèse without light in her cell. Though she was tempted to be frustrated and to fall into self-pity on account of this little inconvenience, Thérèse instead saw it as a grace.

> I felt happy instead of aggrieved, and reflected that poverty consists in being deprived not only of what is convenient, but of what is necessary. And, in this exterior darkness, I found my soul illumined by a brightness that was divine.

She looked for opportunities to embrace "whatever was ugly and inconvenient" rather than to desire the best. For example, when her "pretty little jug" was taken from her cell and was replaced with a "large chipped one," she saw that as a blessing and an opportunity for virtue.

On another occasion, Thérèse was blamed for breaking a small jar that had been left on a window sill. Rather than defend herself, she accepted this false judgment with love. "Without answering, I kissed the ground and promised to be more observant." Though this injustice inflicted upon her was small, it was quite painful for her to embrace. "I was so little advanced in virtue that these small sacrifices cost me dear…" But the cost was not only that of humiliation, it was the price of virtue. She paid the cost and God blessed her with increasing virtue. Though she knew that "at the day of Judgment all would be known," she also knew that all would not be known until then. And it was this small sacrifice, along with many others she embraced each day, that formed her into the saint she became.

Reflection: How well do you embrace small injustices, small sacrifices and small humiliations? Many find these to be quite painful and difficult to accept. But the difficulty often comes because of a failure to see these acts as God sees them. From the divine perspective, small acts of sacrifice have great power to transform the soul and bring forth much virtue and beauty. The more painful the sacrifice, the greater the power to transform.

Reflect upon how quickly you embrace or reject these daily opportunities for virtue. By embracing every small sacrifice quickly and wholeheartedly, you allow God to do great things in your soul. As He does great things, forming you in virtue, your habit of love will grow, and no sacrifice will become too great for you to offer to God.

Dearest Saint Thérèse, your novitiate was a blessed time by which God formed you in so many countless ways. Each small sacrifice you embraced became the source of the increase of your virtue. Pray for me, that I may learn the lesson of these small sacrifices of love. May I imitate your wisdom and see every injustice, sacrifice and humiliation as an invitation to grow in virtue. Saint Thérèse, pray for us.

Chapter Eight

Profession of Sister Thérèse

Lesson Sixty-Seven — Spiritual Poverty

Lesson: Thérèse of the Child Jesus and the Holy Face had hoped to make her profession of vows when she turned seventeen in January 1890. However, she would not be allowed to make her profession until September 8, 1890. Eventually the retreat before her profession arrived and once again, God performed great works in her soul.

> I unconsciously received many interior lights on the best means of pleasing God, and practising virtue. I have often observed that Our Lord will not give me

any store of provisions, but nourishes me each moment with food that is ever new; I find it within me without knowing how it has come there. I simply believe that it is Jesus Himself hidden in my poor heart, who is secretly at work, inspiring me with what He wishes me to do as each occasion arises.

Thérèse continued to discover the new way in which God was forming her in virtue. She did not receive "any store of provisions" on which she could rely during her retreat. But she did discover that God was nourishing her with "food that is ever new." Jesus was secretly transforming her soul and filling her with virtue, oftentimes to her surprise and without her immediate knowledge. Though she was desolate and dry in her spiritual consolations, she was daily perceiving grace at work in her soul by seeing the effects of God's grace.

Thérèse was living a new and beautiful gift of spiritual poverty. She was left empty and wanting, sensing nothing of the presence of God. But in that poverty, she was being nourished, moment by moment by God's providence, with the rich food of grace just prior to professing poverty in her vows.

Reflection: Perhaps, at times, you feel a certain "poverty" in regard to your life of prayer. You may not sense God's presence or perceive His perfect will. If this is on account of idleness in your prayer, then you must grow in fervor. But if your fervor is present and you still find spiritual consolation lacking, you might want to pause and rejoice in that fact.

God often does great things in us, not through powerful feelings and consolations, but through dryness and interior desolation. Though only those who reach the heights of holiness that Thérèse reached experience utter desolation, you might begin to experience it to the extent that you are growing in holiness. This is an invitation to embrace a holy form of spiritual poverty.

Reflect, today, not upon whether you "feel" God's presence in your life. Rather, reflect upon any good fruits you see being born in your life. Where the virtues are, God is at work. Rejoice in that good work and continue to do that which fosters this good fruit.

Dearest Saint Thérèse, God transformed your soul in many ways, despite your loss of all interior consolation. In the midst of this dryness and desolation, God rained down grace upon you, implanting within you the most beautiful virtues. Pray for me, that I may imitate your profound and unwavering commitment to God. May I have that same commitment and be bathed in countless graces from Heaven. Saint Thérèse, pray for us.

Lesson Sixty-Eight — The Devil's Final Attack

Lesson: Oftentimes, when we are on the verge of fulfilling God's glorious will, the devil will lash out in one final act of hatred in an attempt to thwart the good that is about to happen. Though Thérèse's soul was blessed by grace, she had one last test to pass prior to professing her vows and beginning her vocation as a consecrated Carmelite nun.

> On the eve of the great day, instead of being filled with the customary sweetness, my vocation suddenly seemed to me as unreal as a dream. The devil—for it was he—made me feel sure that I was wholly unsuited for life in the Carmel, and that I was deceiving my superiors by entering on a way to which I was not called. The darkness was so bewildering that I understood but one thing—I had no religious vocation, and must return to the world. I cannot describe the agony I endured.

This test, which was permitted by God, was a painful one that struck at the heart of her lifelong mission of giving herself completely to our Lord as His bride. The devil hated what was about to happen and so he was permitted to tempt her with this most vicious attack upon her vocation. God permitted it, knowing full well that she would pass the test.

Thérèse immediately knew she had to share her thoughts and feelings with her sister, who was also her Novice Mistress. She did so and Sister Agnes immediately saw clearly what was happening. Her first reaction was to laugh and then reassure Thérèse that this was nothing other than a temptation to doubt the glorious plan of God. Upon speaking to her and Mother Marie, "the devil was put to instant flight." The devil wanted her to keep this confusion to herself so he could continue to lead her into doubt and despair. When she brought it into the light, the evil one lost all power over her in that moment.

Reflection: Have you ever experienced God leading you toward the fulfillment of His glorious will, only to have last-minute doubts about His will or your ability to fulfill it? This is a common spiritual experience that happens even with everyday situations. Stage fright and panic before a presentation are examples of this.

On a spiritual level, when the "event" we are engaged in is the fulfillment of the will of God, we might often be tempted to turn away and doubt in the last moments. If you experience this in your life, do not see this only as a temptation, see it also as a test that has the potential of solidifying God's will and bringing it to a glorious fulfillment. Discernment must take place slowly, methodically, carefully and prayerfully over time. Trust the test of time rather than quick moments of confusion, panic and doubt. Rely upon the guidance of friends and family in moments of confusion and allow God to speak through them so as to fulfill the glorious plan He has for your life.

Saint Thérèse, you dedicated your whole life to the pursuit of God's will for you to make solemn vows as a Carmelite nun. Though the evil one attempted to derail your vocation one last time, you exposed his menacing temptation to the light by opening your heart to your sister and Mother Superior. Pray for me, that I may be blessed with others who assist me when I face confusion and doubts. May I imitate your hope and perseverance as I seek to fulfill the glorious plan God has for my life. Saint Thérèse, pray for us.

Lesson Sixty-Nine — The Eternal Wedding Feast

Lesson: On September 8, 1890, the Feast of the Nativity of the Blessed Virgin Mary, Little Thérèse professed her vows as a Carmelite nun, becoming Sister Thérèse of the Child Jesus and the Holy Face. In that act, she became solemnly espoused to her Lord and entered into a feast of God's mercy that would only be surpassed by her entrance into Heaven seven years later. From a worldly perspective, Thérèse had given up everything. From a divine perspective, Sister Thérèse now received more than the human mind can fathom.

Since many who knew her in the outside world could not attend this private ceremony (including her father who was too ill), Sister Thérèse decided to send out an invitation to the eternal wedding feast in celebration of her marital union.

> "God Almighty, Creator of Heaven and Earth, Sovereign Ruler of the Universe, and the Glorious Virgin Mary, Queen of the Heavenly Court, announce to you the Spiritual Espousals of their August Son, Jesus, King of Kings and Lord of Lords, with little Thérèse Martin, now Princess and Lady of His Kingdoms of the Holy Childhood and the Passion, assigned to her as a dowry, by her Divine Spouse, from which Kingdoms she holds her titles of nobility—of the Child Jesus and of the Holy Face. It was not possible to invite you to the Wedding Feast which took place on the Mountain of Carmel, September 8, 1890—the Heavenly Court

was alone admitted—but you are requested to be present at the Wedding Feast which will take place tomorrow, the day of Eternity, when Jesus, the Son of God, will come in the clouds of Heaven, in the splendour of His Majesty, to judge the living and the dead.

"The hour being still uncertain, you are asked to hold yourselves in readiness and watch."

This invitation expresses the sheer joy Sister Thérèse felt as she formally began her beautiful vocation. She articulated the eternal spiritual reality of what took place that September morning. She was not caught up in the excitement of the moment alone, she was caught up in the eternal moment. Forever, her espousal to Jesus would be celebrated.

Reflection: It is often very difficult to live in the world without becoming consumed by the desires and temptations of the world. The vocation of Sister Thérèse must teach us to see our own lives from the eternal perspective. How well do you do this? How well do you make daily decisions with your eyes upon Heaven?

God wants us to begin the eternal celebration of our union with Him here and now and to live that way for eternity. We do so when we make daily choices that will be celebrated now and forever in Heaven.

Reflect upon your perspective in life this day. Do you live only for the moment? Or do you live each moment as a preparation for and participation in the eternal joys of Heaven? Let Heaven begin now in your life and, like Sister

Thérèse, your soul will be daily flooded with the peace and joy that surpasses all understanding.

Saint Thérèse, you said "I do" to our Lord and became His beloved spouse for eternity. The joy of that wedding feast was a joy that will be celebrated forever. Pray for me, that I may not live only for the passing pleasures of this world but that I may seek to fully immerse myself in the joys that are eternal. May my Heaven begin now as I say "Yes" to the perfect plan God has for my life. Saint Thérèse, pray for us.

Lesson Seventy — Love More Tender than a Mother's Love

Lesson: Sister Thérèse began her consecrated life with much fervor but also with many interior struggles. At the general retreat following her profession, she suffered greatly and did not know how to explain to others what she endured. She did not even understand it herself.

The priest who led the retreat had a reputation for knowing how to assist sinners but was not very well-known as one who knew how to help nuns. Sister Thérèse, however, found him to be most helpful. She opened her soul to him and he understood her. As they spoke, he reassured her of the tender love God had for her.

> The Father understood me in a marvellous way; he seemed to divine my state, and launched me full sail upon that ocean of confidence and love in which I had longed to advance, but so far had not dared. He told me that my faults did not pain the Good God,

and added: "At this moment I hold His place, and I assure you from Him that He is well pleased with your soul." How happy these consoling words made me!

Perhaps Sister Thérèse still suffered somewhat from the scruples and sensitivity that she had in her earlier years. What she needed was someone who understood her and reassured her that God was pleased with her soul. She feared that her sins displeased God, but fear was not helpful to her spiritual growth. She discovered in this priest the tender love of God, which is more tender than the most tender of mothers. And in that discovery, Sister Thérèse found new life. "My nature is such that fear makes me shrink, while, under love's sweet rule, I not only advance—I fly."

Reflection: Fear, often of judgment, can paralyze us and confuse our thinking. As a result of this fear, we often fail to understand ourselves and God's will for our lives. It is good to have a holy fear of sin, but if our fears become disordered, we fail to fully understand the tender mercy of God.

Do you understand the tender mercy and love of God? Are you able to have a healthy fear of sin while at the same time have great hope in God's love for you and His willingness to forgive?

Ponder your view of sin in your life and seek to imitate Saint Thérèse. She opened her heart to this spiritual father, and he helped her to see her soul as God sees it. Seek the wise counsel of those whom God has put into your life and allow God to speak to you through them. When it is His voice that you hear, you will know it clearly and it will be His voice that sets you free.

Saint Thérèse, you were set free as you came to understand the tender love of the Father in Heaven. In the shadow of His mercy, your sins were put into perspective. Pray for me, that I may have no fear of confessing my sin so that I, too, may come to understand the mercy of God. Saint Thérèse, pray for us.

Lesson Seventy-One — Jesus, Living in Your Soul

Lesson: When Jesus lives in your soul, He directs all your words and actions. At times, He speaks through us to others, and at times He remains silent. It must be our constant duty to speak only the words of Jesus and to be His hands and feet only as He leads.

Such was the case with the Venerable Founder of the Lisieux Carmel, Mother Genevieve of St. Teresa. A couple of months after the general retreat in which Sister Thérèse received many graces, she was graced once again at the passing to Heaven of this holy Mother. A few weeks before her passing, Mother Genevieve saw Sister Thérèse across the room, and Jesus gave her a message for Sister Thérèse as she was leaving the room.

> "Wait, my child, I have just a word for you; you are always asking me for a spiritual bouquet, well, to-day

I give you this one: Serve the Lord in peace and in joy. Remember that Our God is the God of peace."

A week later, Sister Thérèse spoke to Mother Genevieve and asked her if she had another word for her. This time Mother said she did not. But this did not disappoint Sister Thérèse; rather, it inspired her to understand that Jesus was truly living in the soul of Mother Genevieve. If Jesus gave her a word to speak, she spoke it. If He did not, she remained silent.

After Mother Genevieve's death, Sister Thérèse had a dream in which every sister came forward to receive some gift from their Venerable Foundress. Sister Thérèse was last but Mother did not have anything left. Just then, Mother said to Sister Thérèse three times, "To you I leave my heart." Indeed, her heart was the Heart of Christ, and Sister Thérèse did receive this perfect and precious gift.

Reflection: Sometimes, in our desire to do good and to help those around us, we can offer all forms of "advice" and guidance. But are the words you speak and the actions you perform from you or from the heart of Christ? Holiness consists in being so conformed to the Heart of Christ that He and He alone lives within you and speaks and acts through you. This takes a true discipline of love to allow our Lord to use you in such a careful way.

Reflect upon Jesus living in you, acting through you and speaking His words of love in the words of your mouth. Pray that you may be so united to Him that He and He alone is the actor of your soul.

Saint Thérèse, you were blessed with the holy example of Mother Genevieve. She enfleshed the Heart of Christ and spoke only His words of love. Pray for me, that I may be blessed with such holy witnesses in my life. May I also seek to receive the Heart of Christ and allow His Heart to dictate all I say and do. Saint Thérèse, pray for us.

Lesson Seventy-Two — Adorning Heaps of Rubbish

Lesson: Toward the end of 1891, the Carmel convent of Lisieux experienced an epidemic of influenza that took the lives of several sisters. Those who did not become ill suffered greatly as they offered these sisters to God. Sister Thérèse herself was ill only briefly, but in spite of these earthly trials around her, Sister Thérèse grew in her love of Jesus.

After the influenza epidemic passed, she continued to receive much interior consolation from Jesus on a daily basis. However, she had the opposite experience every time she received Jesus in Holy Communion. Instead of experiencing the closeness of God in Holy Communion, Sister Thérèse felt nothing of His presence, even though she prayed with much fervor.

Despite the lack of consolations, the way Sister Thérèse prepared for Holy Communion reveals her deep faith.

> I picture my soul as a piece of waste ground and beg Our Blessed Lady to take away my imperfections——

which are as heaps of rubbish—and to build upon it a splendid tabernacle worthy of Heaven, and adorn it with her own adornments. Then I invite all the Angels and Saints to come and sing canticles of love, and it seems to me that Jesus is well pleased to see Himself received so grandly, and I share in His joy. But all this does not prevent distractions and drowsiness from troubling me, and not unfrequently I resolve to continue my thanksgiving throughout the day, since I made it so badly in choir.

Sister Thérèse was unwavering in her faith every time she received Holy Communion. The loss of consolation at that time was an invitation from Jesus to receive Him NOT because she was consoled, but because He was God and was worthy of her love.

However, one day she grew spiritually weary and for several days had only received a small part of the host because there were not enough. In her wearied state, she decided that on the next day, if there were not enough hosts, this would be a sign that Jesus did not want to come to the "heaps of rubbish" that made up her soul. But Jesus, in His tender care, inspired the priest that day to give Sister Thérèse two full hosts, which she understood to be an act of great mercy from Jesus in the moment that she needed to be reminded of His love.

Reflection: God knows what we need and when we need it. Sister Thérèse faithfully received Holy Communion, making a profound act of faith in her thanksgiving day after day without any sense of God's presence. The moment

Sister Thérèse began to waver out of weakness and doubt, God revealed His love and His desire to come to her.

Ponder these two powerful lessons from Sister Thérèse. First, it is our duty to love God for the sake of God alone. He is worthy of our love, and we must love Him even when we do not feel that love. Second, God will never abandon us. In our weakness, when we need His presence the most, He will be there.

Commit yourself, today, to fidelity to Jesus no matter how you feel. Say "Yes" to Him when you are desolate, and say "Yes" when you are consoled. If you are faithful through all things, you can be certain that God's fidelity will be repaid in abundance.

Saint Thérèse, in faith you pondered the reality that all you have to offer Jesus is a "heap of rubbish" within your soul. But in faith, you trusted that your soul would be transformed into Jesus' glorious throne. Pray for me, that I may love God in good times and in difficult ones. May I imitate your faith and devotion and never waver in my love of God for the sake of love alone. Saint Thérèse, pray for us.

Lesson Seventy-Three — A Tear is Shed with Strength and Love

Lesson: Thérèse's father, Saint Louis Martin, suffered greatly after returning home from a three-year hospital stay. He had to be cared for by Céline and Léonie for the two years prior to his death. During this time, he was only once able to visit his other daughters in the Carmel Convent. In that final visit, he lovingly looked at his little Queen Thérèse and said only one thing, "In Heaven!" as he pointed upward. From that time onward, Mr. Martin was incapacitated in body and mind and his former self was now veiled with the face of our suffering Lord.

Sister Thérèse loved him dearly and continually wrote to Céline and Léonie to encourage them in their duties to care for their father. Throughout this great suffering and deep sorrow, Sister Thérèse remained strong. Her disposition taught that strength, peace, joy, suffering and sorrow were not in conflict. Even though it meant she would no longer see her father in this world, Thérèse longed for him to be in Heaven. One sister recalled Sister Thérèse speaking about her father with perfect serenity and peace, while at the same time shedding a large tear from her eye. This was a lesson to her of the strength of Sister Thérèse's soul, as well as her deep affection for her suffering father. Love and suffering were commingled within her heart.

Sister Thérèse's devotion to the Holy Face was a great consolation to her at this time of her father's suffering. Her reflection on the Holy Face was a constant image of her father, whose suffering veiled his former self. From the time of her profession until the time of his passing on July 29, 1894, Thérèse's father and the Holy Face of Jesus were one and the same. This was Mr. Martin's final gift to his little Queen.

Reflection: In each of our lives we will be given a cross that is hard to carry but is also clearly God's will. Reflect upon the losses you have experienced in life, which God has asked you to accept with courage, strength, love and sorrow.

If you live in the past and refuse to let go of the blessings of the past, you will fail to allow those blessings to become transformed into even greater blessings. As Sister Thérèse endured the slow deterioration of her father on Earth, she discovered the suffering face of Jesus and was given her Beloved in exchange for one who was so beloved to her.

Ponder the experience that Sister Thérèse must have felt. Allow her experience to direct any loss that you have encountered. Allow her hope and strength to be a guiding light for your own journey.

Saint Thérèse, for five years you slowly witnessed the physical and mental deterioration of your loving king. But his last gift to you, in his suffering, was to deepen your knowledge of your Heavenly King. Pray for me, that I may find Jesus in every sorrow I endure, especially in the sorrow I endure on account of the suffering of those I love. Saint Thérèse, pray for us.

Lesson Seventy-Four — Overcoming "Insurmountable" Obstacles

Lesson: Though Céline also felt a call to follow her sisters into holy espousal with Jesus at the Lisieux Carmel, God called her to care for her father during his illness. Léonie assisted her for the first year their father returned to Lisieux but then entered the Visitation Convent in Caen at her second attempt at religious life. Céline faithfully cared for their father with the help of their uncle, a maid and a male assistant. When their beloved father passed to his Heavenly reward on July 29, 1894, Céline was now free to turn her eyes to Carmel.

> Now that he was with God, the last ties which kept his consoling Angel in the world were broken. Angels do not remain on this earth; when they have accomplished their mission, they return instantly to Heaven. That is why they have wings. Céline tried therefore to fly to the Carmel, but the obstacles seemed insurmountable.

One obstacle came from Father Pichon who wanted Céline to go to Canada to help him found a new apostolate. Other obstacles included the opposition of Canon Delatroette who did not believe it wise that four Martin sisters be in the same Carmel. Several of the sisters at the Lisieux Carmel also were concerned about having four sisters together. Her cousin Jeanne La Neele and her husband Francis wanted Céline to remain in the world rather than waste her life at Carmel. Eventually, the only opposing voice was Sister Aimee of Jesus, one of the Carmelite nuns, so Sister Thérèse turned to prayer that she would have a change of heart.

> God, Who holds in His Hand the hearts of His creatures, and inclines them as He will, deigned in His infinite mercy and ineffable condescension to change that Sister's mind. She was the first person I met after my thanksgiving, and, with tears in her eyes, she spoke of Céline's entrance, which she now

ardently desired. Shortly afterwards the Bishop set every obstacle aside, and then you were able, dear Mother, without any hesitation, to open our doors to the poor little exile.

Sister Thérèse's prayers were successful and this final desire of hers, that her sister Céline join her at Carmel, was now set to be fulfilled. Céline embraced her calling and followed Pauline, Marie and Thérèse to Carmel on September 14, 1894.

Reflection: Have you encountered obstacles in the fulfillment of God's will that appear to be "insurmountable?" Oftentimes God allows us to face such challenges to purify our intentions and to strengthen our resolve. Céline and Thérèse only wanted the will of God to be done, but they discovered that those who were closest to them placed one obstacle after another. Family, priests and other religious sisters were standing in the way of the will of God.

Whenever you discern the will of God but find it difficult to fulfill, prayer is the key. Reflect upon anything that poses a great challenge to you today. Do all you can to embrace the will of God, but know that only God can open doors and, at times, move mountains. Trust in the power of prayer and you will see God's will come to fruition.

Saint Thérèse, you supported your sister Céline in the fulfillment of her vocation, but you both were met with what appeared to be insurmountable obstacles. As a result, you entrusted all to prayer and God changed hearts. Pray for me, that I may never be a hinderance to the fulfillment of the will of God in my life and in the lives of others.

May I also have the deepest trust in God and entrust all things to Him through prayer. Saint Thérèse, pray for us.

Lesson Seventy-Five — My Last Desire

Lesson: Sister Thérèse had desired many things in life. She desired to enter Carmel at an early age, the well-being of her father in his illness, that Céline follow her to Carmel and many other smaller desires along the way. Once Céline entered Carmel, it was as if every hope and desire Sister Thérèse had in life had been fulfilled. All earthly ties had been severed, and she was able to begin a new focus in her life. She turned to the last desire of her heart, which would become the single desire for which she would now live. She desired to love God and God alone.

> Now I have no desire left, unless it be to love Jesus even unto folly! It is Love alone that draws me...From earliest childhood I have imagined that the Little Flower would be gathered in its springtime; now, the spirit of self-abandonment alone is my guide. I have no other compass, and know not how to ask anything with eagerness, save the perfect accomplishment of God's designs upon my soul.

Sister Thérèse turned her eyes to love and love alone. Self-abandonment to the Heart of Christ was the only mission of her life.

> The Science of Love! How sweetly do these words echo in my soul! That science alone do I desire.

Having given all my substance for it, like the Spouse in the Canticles, "I think that I have given nothing." (St. John of the Cross, Cant. 8:7) After so many graces, may I not sing with the Psalmist that "the Lord is good, that His Mercy endureth for ever?" (Psalm 103(104):1)

Reflection: Most people are distracted by the desires, busyness, temptations and needs of daily life. Life can seem complex and even complicated. There are many distractions that draw us here and there, competing for our time, attention and desires. Though we are not all called to follow Saint Thérèse into a cloister so as to be able to turn our singular focus to the love of God, we must seek to imitate her as we live in the world.

Reflect upon the desires of your heart. What is it that you long for, think about and perhaps even obsess over? All Christians must seek to surrender their desires in life to God so that they will all be directed in accord with His perfect will. The more we do that, the more we love God. And the more we love God, the more we fulfill His perfect will in every aspect of our lives.

Saint Thérèse, you were given a special vocation in which you could devote all your time and energy to the love of God alone. Pray for me, that I may imitate your love and that I may do all things for God's glory so as to abandon myself into His perfect will for my life. May every desire of my heart be purified and directed by the love of our most Merciful God. Saint Thérèse, pray for us.

Lesson Seventy-Six — A "Victim" to Merciful Love

Lesson: As Sister Thérèse turned her eyes to the love of God alone, God began to teach her many lessons in the depths of her soul. On June 9, 1895, the year after Céline entered Carmel, Sister Thérèse was pondering the unique vocation given to some to become a victim of God's justice. She realized that some people are given the mysterious vocation of suffering greatly for sinners so as to free them from the punishments necessitated by God's justice. But in pondering this noble vocation of victimhood, she immediately became aware of the need to become a "victim" in a new way. She suddenly discovered that she was to be a *Victim of God's Merciful Love.*

> O my Divine Master, shall Thy Justice alone receive victims of holocaust? Has not Thy Merciful Love also need thereof?...
>
> O my God! must Thy Love which is disdained lie hidden in Thy Heart? Methinks, if Thou shouldst find souls offering themselves as victims of holocaust to Thy Love, Thou wouldst consume them rapidly; Thou wouldst be well pleased to suffer the flames of infinite tenderness to escape that are imprisoned in Thy Heart.
>
> If Thy Justice—which is of earth—must needs be satisfied, how much more must Thy Merciful Love desire to inflame souls, since *"Thy mercy reacheth even to the Heavens?"* (Cf. Psalm 35[36]:6) O Jesus! Let me

> be that happy victim—consume Thy holocaust with the Fire of Divine Love!"

In this revelation, Sister Thérèse discovered one of the greatest mysteries of faith ever discovered. From the moment she responded to that discovery and offered herself as a "Victim of Merciful Love," her life was forever transformed.

> Every moment this Merciful Love renews me and purifies me, leaving in my soul no trace of sin. I cannot fear Purgatory; I know I do not merit to enter, even, into that place of expiation with the Holy Souls, but I also know that the fire of Love is more sanctifying than the fire of Purgatory. I know that Jesus could not wish useless suffering for us, and He would not inspire me with the desires I feel, were He not willing to fulfill them.

Reflection: This discovery on the part of Sister Thérèse is a profound mystery. God's justice, and His punishment for all sin, is only transformed by love. When one loves God, and makes a complete offering of one's life to the love of God, God is bound to remove all sin and all stain of sin.

If this discovery on the part of Sister Thérèse seems beyond your comprehension, do not worry. She did not discover it fully until after being a consecrated nun for several years. Therefore, instead of worrying about how fully you understand this mystery of victimhood to divine love, ponder the fact that love of God is so profound and so deep that you will be pondering it for all eternity.

Allow the vocation of Saint Thérèse to intrigue you, to call to you and to inspire you to seek more in your relationship with God. Love of God is tangible, real and transforming. It is not a lofty idea; it is a practical reality. Pray that you, like Sister Thérèse, will be open to the mystery of this love and will allow it to transform you forever.

Dearest Saint Thérèse, you offered yourself to Jesus as a victim to His divine love. In so doing, you were sanctified and freed from all sin, remaining perfectly in His merciful Heart. Pray for me, that I may come to understand the love of God and that I, too, may offer myself to Him as a spotless victim of love. Saint Thérèse, pray for us.

Chapter Nine

Life as a Religious Sister

Notebook for Mother Marie de Gonzague — Manuscript C

June–July 1897

Lesson Seventy-Seven — Detachment

Lesson: The first eight chapters of the *Story of a Soul* were written by Sister Thérèse when she was only twenty-two years old, from January 1895 until January 20, 1896. Upon reading this first manuscript, Sister Agnes of Jesus (Pauline) was attentive to the fact that little of Sister Thérèse's life as a nun was included in her writing. Most of the content focused on her childhood up until her profession of vows. Since Sister Agnes was no longer prioress, she went to Mother Marie de Gonzague and asked her to order Sister Thérèse to write more, this time focusing on her life as a religious sister. Mother Marie did just that. Therefore, during the months of June and July of 1897, just a few months before she would die at the age of twenty-four, Sister Thérèse took up the pen again and continued writing about her life as a religious sister. Out of holy obedience, she shared her heart and all that Jesus taught her. She began this section of her autobiography with the following:

> Dear Mother, I thought I had written enough, and now you wish for more details of my religious life. I will not argue, but I cannot help smiling when I have to tell you things that you know quite as well as I do. Nevertheless, I will obey. I do not ask what use this manuscript can be to any one, I assure you that even were you to burn it before my eyes, without having read it, I should not mind in the least.

It's important to note, once again, that Sister Thérèse wrote out of obedience, not to glorify her own soul. Additionally, she was beautifully detached from what she wrote: "even were you to burn it before my eyes, without having read it, I should not mind in the least." Imagine if Mother Marie were to burn her manuscript, right before the eyes of Sister Thérèse, without even reading it. For most people, this would strike deeply at their pride and would be the cause of sorrow and even anger. But it wouldn't have been the case with Sister Thérèse.

Though that is not what happened to this second manuscript, ponder the possibility of Sister Thérèse witnessing such an act. Perhaps some small sin of pride would have arisen, but her heart was so detached from vanity and the opinion of others that she would have quickly rejoiced in such a humiliation. She would have rejoiced that God gave her such a grace to act in holy obedience and that only the angels and saints would have seen all she wrote.

Reflection: How would you react if you were asked to pour out your heart on paper and then all you wrote was burned before it was ever read? Have you shared your heart with another, only to be ignored or misunderstood? This is a common struggle and can be the cause of hurt and sorrow.

It's important to understand that, even though it is not virtuous for another to dismiss the content of our heart and show little interest in what we share, our peace of soul ought not depend upon another's reaction. We must seek to have the same detachment from the listening ear of another as Sister Thérèse had in regard to her manuscript. If the sharing of her soul was read, understood and loved by one or by many, so be it. If her sharing was burned and left unread, so be it.

Reflect upon how attached you are to the interest or disinterest that others take in you. Certainly it is a blessing of love when another takes interest in you and wants to understand you. But unless you can view others' reactions to you with detachment, your sharing will not be a freely-given gift.

Sister Thérèse did not write with the expectation that others would benefit from what she wrote nor did she do so for attention or vainglory. She wrote out of obedience and love, and this total gift of her soul was ultimately received by many and continues to be received by many more today.

Dearest Saint Thérèse, you shared your heart freely and openly, for Jesus truly lived within you and His love shone through you. Pray for me, that I may willingly share all that God has done in my life with those who seek to understand. May I also have patience and detachment from this act of love so that I will share only that which our Lord inspires me to share. Saint Thérèse, pray for us.

Lesson Seventy-Eight — Holy Indifference

Lesson: As Sister Thérèse grew in holiness, those around her began to perceive her as a pure soul who was living in the Heart of Christ. Her holiness radiated, and those who had the eyes of faith could see this. Mother Marie was difficult on her at times but for Sister Thérèse's own good. It was an act of love so that Sister Thérèse would not grow proud. Mother Marie also expressed her love and respect for Sister Thérèse, and she manifested much confidence in her genuine holiness. Additionally, various other sisters, as well as associates of the convent, were aware of the spiritual depth and beauty of this Little Flower of God. How did Sister Thérèse respond to this?

When I say that I am indifferent to praise, I am not speaking, dear Mother, of the love and confidence you show me; on the contrary I am deeply touched thereby, but I feel that I have now nothing to fear, and I can listen to those praises unperturbed, attributing to God all that is good in me. If it please Him to make me appear better than I am, it is nothing to me, He can act as He will.

Sister Thérèse had such a deep love of God that His "opinion" was all that mattered, since His opinion was Truth itself. As for the admiration and praise of others, this was deeply touching to Sister Thérèse, since their love and affection was an act of the tender Heart of God. But she also had a "holy indifference" to the opinions of others, even when those opinions were good opinions.

Sister Thérèse teaches us the beautiful lesson that we must be truly indifferent to others' praises if we are to be able to receive their love and affection in a meaningful way. Holy indifference means we do not depend upon what others say or think, but when others are drawn to our virtue, we rejoice at the expression of love they share. Only if we have a holy indifference can we receive the love and even praise of another with humility and joy.

Reflection: Do you seek the praise and admiration of others? Do you allow yourself to become dependent upon what others think about you or even say about you? This can be a heavy burden to carry and will always leave you feeling unsatisfied.

On the contrary, if you seek to have a holy indifference in your relationships, you will find that every shared act of love will be a joy. However, if you do not receive praise and affection, you will not be disappointed. Holy indifference is essential to every relationship of love. Without it, freedom is lost and selfishness determines our decisions.

Reflect upon your relationships, especially your closest ones. Pray that your praise for them will be purely for the sake of love and not for any selfish motive. It's true that when another gives you praise, you are blessed. But be careful not to count on this or make the praise or lack thereof determine your response. Seek a holy detachment, so that all that is given and received will be free and holy.

Dearest Saint Thérèse, you did not allow your actions to become contingent upon the praise of others. If they loved you and praised you, that was fine. If they did not, that was fine also. Pray for me that I may discover and live this beautiful and mysterious virtue of holy indifference. May I seek to love for the sake of love alone. Saint Thérèse, pray for us.

Lesson Seventy-Nine — Discovery of the "Little Way"

Lesson: Sister Thérèse spent the last two years of her life discovering and sharing the deepest wisdom of God. One gift that she discovered within her soul was a desire to become a saint. And though she realized that she could not do this on her own, she also understood that "God would not inspire desires which could not be realised…"

Therefore, Sister Thérèse set out on the mission of discovering how God would enable her to become a great saint, despite her littleness and weakness.

She pondered how an elevator was much easier and quicker than climbing stairs and that an elevator was necessary for those who were weak. Similarly, if she were to ascend to the heights of holiness, she would need a spiritual lift to Heaven. Her reflection on Scripture led her to conclude that this lift was received by becoming little and clinging to the arms of Jesus.

> Thine Arms, then, O Jesus, are the lift which must raise me up even unto Heaven. To get there I need not grow; on the contrary, I must remain little, I must become still less.

Sister Thérèse's new way was to embrace her littleness, weakness and nothingness. She had nothing on her own that could make her a saint. Therefore, if she could remain weak and little, like a little child, she reasoned that she would cling to Jesus in love and never let go. Though she was a sinner, God's justice could not condemn her if she became small and weak. God would have no choice but to carry her to holiness and bring her to heights higher than she could ever imagine. A child is blind to its weakness when in the arms of a parent. It is trusting and is carried wherever the parent decides. Therefore, with complete confidence, Sister Thérèse concluded that this was the best and simplest way, the "Little Way," to become holy. This is the path of "littleness" and centers on the perfect trust of a child.

Reflection: Too often we pride ourselves on our virtue and strength. We allow ourselves to believe that whatever we set our minds to, we can accomplish. But are you able to achieve holiness on your own? Does not your sin already condemn you before the justice of God? Not if you turn your full attention to the merciful love of Jesus.

Holiness is a gift, and Sister Thérèse, in her humility, knew she was incapable of attaining it on her own. Therefore, she sought to become little, to become "nothing." Only in such weakness would she become irresistible to Jesus who would then carry her to the highest heights of holiness.

Reflect upon your own attitude toward holiness. Do you fall into the trap of thinking that you can attain this by your own effort? Ponder the "Little Way" of this saint of God and know that it is the best way for you. Discover your weakness and nothingness and make a claim on the mercy of Jesus to carry you in your need. If you imitate this humble trust of Saint Thérèse, you, too, will have discovered this little way of love.

Dearest Saint Thérèse, you discovered that becoming little, dependent and weak enabled you to make a claim on Jesus, abandoning yourself into His merciful love. Your trust was not on account of your own merit, it was because of the infinite love of God. Pray for me, that I may imitate your "Little Way" and may seek to become little and weak before the infinite mercy of God. Saint Thérèse, pray for us.

Lesson Eighty — "Feed My Lambs"

Lesson: Though she was young, Sister Thérèse was given the responsibility of leading the novices, but she asked Mother Superior not to give her the title "Novice Mistress." She happily obliged and Sister Thérèse committed herself to the formation of her sisters.

> You have said to me, as Our Lord said to St. Peter: "Feed my lambs." I am amazed, for I feel that I am so little. I have entreated you to feed your little lambs yourself and to keep me among them. You have complied in part with my reasonable wish, and have called me their companion, rather than their mistress, telling me nevertheless to lead them through fertile and shady pastures, to point out where the grass is sweetest and best, and warn them against the brilliant but poisonous flowers, which they must never touch except to crush under foot.

Sister Thérèse was amazed at this responsibility but embraced it as well as she could. It was her responsibility "to lead them through fertile and shady pastures, to point out where the grass is sweetest and best, and warn them against the brilliant but poisonous flowers, which they must never touch except to crush under foot."

Mother Superior understood that the Divine Master had enlightened the soul of Sister Thérèse and given her the experience of years. This was one of the reasons she appointed Sister Thérèse to this responsibility. Given this assurance of her inner character, Sister Thérèse still realized that she could lead these novices only if she remained "little" and "wholly dependent" upon the mercy of God. God and God alone would lead His little flock through her.

> How is it, dear Mother, that my youth and inexperience have not frightened you? Are you not afraid that I shall let your lambs stray afar? In acting as you have done, perhaps you remembered that Our Lord is often pleased to give wisdom to little ones.

Her youth and inexperience were not hindrances to Sister Thérèse; rather, they were the qualities she needed to be used so well by God. She led with tender love, firmness and mercy. Her little lambs opened their hearts to her motherly care.

Reflection: It can be difficult to exercise discipline and tender love at the same time. Sister Thérèse did this well. How about you? Over whom has God given you responsibility? With whom have you been entrusted the task of acting as a shepherd?

When exercising authority over others, there are many pitfalls we may encounter. Some long to be "liked" so badly that they are fearful of being firm, and they give in to pressure almost immediately. Others are harsh and overly judgmental or condemning and thus abuse their authority.

Reflect upon the ideal balance of strength and tenderness, discipline and mercy, correction and forgiveness. Reflect also upon those for whom you have been given a certain moral responsibility in life. Perhaps you have civil authority,

Church authority, authority within your family or authority at work. Authority means you must lead and "shepherd" in accord with the mind and heart of Christ. Ponder Saint Thérèse and seek to imitate her heart as she sought to imitate the heart of the Shepherd.

Dearest Saint Thérèse, you loved your "little lambs" and sought to exercise a true motherly heart over them. You perceived the uniqueness of each one and loved each as she needed. Pray for me, that I may also exercise an authority of love over those whom God has entrusted to my care. May I imitate the Good Shepherd and lead my own "little flock" toward the Kingdom of God. Saint Thérèse, pray for us.

Lesson Eighty-One — A Joyful Announcement

Lesson: The year leading up to Lent of 1896, when Sister Thérèse was between the ages of 22 and 23, she suffered a deeper interior martyrdom than could ever be described. Exteriorly, most people would have never imagined that Sister Thérèse had suffered. In fact, most would have considered her as one who never tasted suffering. However, she recalled to Mother Marie, "If the martyrdom which I have endured for the past year were made known, how astonished everyone would be!"

This interior suffering that she endured enabled her to face her final martyrdom with much joy and anticipation. On April 2, 1896, the night of Holy Thursday, Sister Thérèse wanted to remain all night in prayer with our Lord, but she was denied permission to do so. Therefore, she returned to her cell and put out the light. Just then, as Sister Thérèse lay down to sleep, she felt what she described as a "hot stream" rise to her lips. She felt blood coming from her lungs, the first sign of her imminent death from tuberculosis. But her interior martyrdom of the past year prepared her for this physical martyrdom so well that she received this "hot stream" as a truly joyful announcement.

> At five o'clock, when it was time to get up, I remembered at once that I had some good news to learn, and going to the window I found, as I had expected, that our handkerchief was soaked with blood. Dearest Mother, what hope was mine! I was firmly convinced that on this anniversary of His Death, my Beloved had allowed me to hear His first call, like a sweet, distant murmur, heralding His joyful approach.

Most people who suddenly become aware of a serious illness would react with disbelief, denial, fear or anxiety. But Sister Thérèse was so consumed by the love of God that she saw this as a gift to be with her Lord very soon. She continued her daily routine and entered into all the austerities of Holy Week with vigor and fidelity. Through it all, she fixed her eyes upon her Lord and anticipated her great day: "the hope of soon entering Heaven transported me with joy."

Such a joyful, inviting attitude toward one's own impending death is an attitude rarely seen. Very few people love God with such passion that they are "transported with joy" at the thought of their imminent demise. Sister Thérèse was one of those rare souls.

Reflection: How would you react if you were to find out today that you have a terminal illness? This is a "heavy" question to say the least. Few would react as Sister Thérèse did because few are as fully given over to the love of God as she was. Though you might not immediately react to the news of your impending death as Sister Thérèse did, you can still reflect upon her joyous reaction and learn from it.

Death is not frightening to those who love God and trust Him with every fiber of their being. If you find yourself somewhat frightened at the thought of death, do not worry. Instead, use this meditation as an opportunity to ponder why you would not react to such an announcement as Sister Thérèse did. What is it you fear about death? Why do you fear? Do you long to be with God in Heaven? Do you trust Him to care for your loved ones if you were to go to Him soon?

Ponder these questions in faith and hope. God and God alone is the author of life and, thus, He and He alone determines when and how we pass. We must always be ready, watching, waiting and anticipating this great day with joy. That can only be accomplished if we love and trust God with our whole being.

Dearest Saint Thérèse, your mind and heart were so consumed with the love of God that this first "announcement" of your pending death was received with incredible joy. Pray for me, that I may love and trust God so deeply that I will fear nothing in life, not even death. May I be filled with hope in all things and anticipate the glorious gift of being with our Divine Lord forever in Heaven. Saint Thérèse, pray for us.

Lesson Eighty-Two — The Land of Fog

Lesson: Shortly after receiving much joy and consolation at the thought of soon being in Heaven with her Lord, Sister Thérèse received a different interior gift: months of interior suffering and darkness.

> ...the thought of Heaven, which had consoled me from my earliest childhood, now became a subject of conflict and torture....I wish I could express what I feel, but it is beyond me. One must have passed through this dark tunnel to understand its blackness.

In her attempt to explain what she went through, she offered a metaphor. She explained that the world we are in is a land of fog. We live here, unable to see, but have been told that this is not our land and that there is a glorious and beautiful land to which we will be taken one day. The thought and anticipation of such a land filled Sister Thérèse with great delight. She looked forward to Heaven!

However, for these months of interior darkness, Sister Thérèse no longer dreamt of Heaven and the Land filled with Light. Instead, all she heard in her soul was the lie of the evil one:

> "You dream of a land of light and fragrance, you dream that the Creator of these wonders will be

yours for ever, you think one day to escape from these mists where you now languish. Nay, rejoice in death, which will give you, not what you hope for, but a night darker still, the night of utter nothingness!"

This lie echoed over and over in her mind during these months of darkness. While most people would see this as an awful experience, Sister Thérèse understood it as a precious gift from God. Why would God allow her to be stripped of all sensible hope of Heaven? Because this loss of all interior consolation provided her an opportunity to deepen her faith. And that is exactly what happened.

I have made more acts of Faith in this last year than during all the rest of my life. Each time that my enemy would provoke me to combat, I behave as a gallant soldier. I know that a duel is an act of cowardice, and so, without once looking him in the face, I turn my back on the foe, then I hasten to my Saviour, and vow that I am ready to shed my blood in witness of my belief in Heaven. I tell him, if only He will deign to open it to poor unbelievers, I am content to sacrifice all pleasure in the thought of it as long as I live.

Thus, the loss of all interior delights and the loss of all joy of Heaven did not discourage Sister Thérèse. On the contrary, this desolation afforded her the opportunity to make the most pure and most profound act of faith possible. This act of faith was a true martyrdom of spirit.

Reflection: How easily are you controlled by your feelings? Sister Thérèse felt nothing but loss and interior suffering. Her feelings were dry, dead and painful, but this did not lead her to doubt or despair. She did not turn away from God as a result of this interior suffering. Rather, she used it as an opportunity to make a profound act of faith in God and in Heaven, despite how she felt. How well would you endure such a test?

Oftentimes we base our decisions on how we feel, rather than on what we know. Sister Thérèse knew, in the darkness and silence of faith, that Heaven was real and that she loved God and had perfect hope of being with Him in Heaven. God, in His abundant mercy, allowed Sister Thérèse to manifest this profound faith by stripping her of all interior consolation, so that the manifestation of her faith, hope and love were pure.

Reflect upon how easily you allow your feelings, or lack of feelings, to determine how you live. Reflect, especially, on how what you feel controls your life of virtue and love of God. Seek to imitate the freewill choice this saint manifested so that you, too, will be purified in your virtue.

Dearest Saint Thérèse, in good times and in difficult ones, including the most painful interior desolations, you chose to love God, have hope in Heaven and believe in Him with unwavering faith. Pray for me, that I may imitate your beautiful virtue and may never be controlled by the feelings I experience in life. May I love for the sake of love, believe for the sake of faith, and hope for the sake of hope. Saint Thérèse, pray for us.

Lesson Eighty-Three — "I am Free"

Lesson: Freedom is rarely understood in its purest form. So often, freedom is understood to be the freedom *to do what I want* rather than the freedom *to do what I ought*. True freedom means that one's soul is stripped of all that hinders it in its rise toward God and that there are no obstacles to faith, hope and love.

Sister Thérèse discovered that the "dark night" of deep interior suffering was the greatest gift God could give her because it was through this suffering that her soul was purified and her virtues pruned. Thus, during these months of her life, she wrote some of the most beautiful poetry to God. These poems were an expression of her soul only because her love became so deeply purified by her interior suffering. They were not an expression of any interior consolation.

> No doubt, dear Mother, you will think I exaggerate somewhat *the night of my soul*. If you judge by the poems I have composed this year, it must seem as though I have been flooded with consolations, like a child for whom the veil of Faith is almost rent asunder. And yet it is not a veil—it is a wall which rises to the very heavens and shuts out the starry sky.

It took several years before Sister Thérèse was ready to enter into this final purification of her soul prior to her earthly death. But in this purification, God took every natural longing of her heart away, and she was left to sing the mercies of the Lord on the level of pure virtue.

In this purification, Sister Thérèse also discovered something that we all seek. She discovered freedom: freedom from suffering, freedom from fear, and freedom from everything but love of God.

> Dear Mother, it seems to me that at present there is nothing to impede my upward flight, for I have no longer any desire save to love Him till I die. I am free; I fear nothing now...

She was free. She was free of all desires other than a desire for God. She was free from all fear in that nothing worried her, not even the most painful suffering. To her, all was sweet and all things became part of her Little Way to Heaven. Nothing of this world and nothing from the evil one could stand in her way. Her freedom was on a level that very few ever attain.

Reflection: What is your concept of freedom? Is it that of Sister Thérèse? Probably not. Sister Thérèse discovered a freedom that few discover. She found freedom from everything except love of God. She did not fear suffering, or death, or life, or anything. She suffered greatly and chose love in the midst of that suffering to such a degree that suffering no longer afflicted her. All she knew was love.

Reflect upon your attitude toward the suffering you endure. Do you see suffering as undesirable and as an obstacle toward the fulfillment of your happiness in life? Seek to discover the wisdom of the Little Flower and make continual acts of love, despite all you suffer in life. Know that every suffering has the potential to become a glorious gift that will help you discover what it means to be truly free to love and free from all that hinders love.

Dearest Saint Thérèse, you discovered the hidden, mysterious and painful road to freedom. Love in the face of all suffering was the one and only way to be rid of all suffering and to find joy in all things. Pray for me, that I may be inspired by the discovery you made and attain the level of love you had for God. May I find freedom as I love and join you in singing the endless mercies of the Lord. Saint Thérèse, pray for us.

Lesson Eighty-Four — "My Consent was All He Desired"

Lesson: In 1861, the Carmelite sisters of Lisieux embraced a missionary spirit and sent four sisters to Saigon (Vietnam) to begin a new Carmel. From that convent, many other convents were founded in the far East.

In 1895, a professed sister of Saigon, Sister Anne of the Sacred Heart, spent time in Lisieux hoping that some of the sisters of Lisieux would return with her to Saigon and from there found a Carmelite convent in Hanoï. Sister Thérèse herself was a perfect candidate, except for her deteriorating health. After much discussion, however, the superiors did not permit anyone's departure.

In pondering the possibility of moving so far from the comforts of home in Lisieux, Sister Thérèse understood that if she were healed and moved to Hanoï, she would be making quite a sacrifice. In Lisieux, she was known and loved so deeply. If she were to move to Hanoï, she would be sacrificing the comforts of this love. Though she was never given the opportunity to choose this sacrifice on account of her health, she chose it in her heart and offered the sacrifice of all the love she gave and received at her little heaven in Lisieux.

> Here, I am loved by you and all the Sisters, and this love is very sweet to me, and I dream of a convent where I should be unknown, where I should taste the bitterness of exile. I know only too well how useless I am, and so it is not for the sake of the services I might render to the Carmel of Hanoï that I would leave all that is dearest to me—my sole reason would be to do God's Will, and sacrifice myself for Him.

At this time in her life, Sister Thérèse's only desire was to offer herself to God as a sacrifice of love. She sought every bitter chalice she could drink because it was in these sacrifices that her soul was purified and her love was strengthened. Sister Thérèse firmly resolved to say "Yes" to such a mission if her health improved. However, upon making an interior consent, she soon realized that her health would not improve. This was a victory for grace, nonetheless, because her "Yes" was all that God wanted. She would stay in Lisieux until she died, but her willing sacrifice sufficed as a source of much grace.

Reflection: When you think of the sacrifices that God might want you to make, do you embrace them willingly? Or do you rationalize and come up with many reasons to avoid these sacrifices? Sacrifice often appears unpleasant at first. But when we see sacrifice as it truly is, as an act of pure love, then we, like Saint Thérèse, will joyfully seek out every sacrifice God invites us to make.

Reflect upon any sacrifice in your life that you have been avoiding. Why are you avoiding it? Try to look at that sacrifice not as something painful, but as something beautiful you can offer to God. Resolve firmly, in faith, to say "Yes" to anything God asks of you and strive to do so without any hesitancy at all. Sacrifice is at the heart of love, and love is what you were made for.

Dearest Saint Thérèse, you were blessed to see every sacrifice in life as an opportunity for love. The initial pain of each sacrifice was overshadowed by the beauty and power of love. Pray for me, that I may learn to love with a pure heart and that I will say "Yes" to every sacrifice God asks of me. May I, like you, learn to love beyond the hurt and find joy in the total and selfless gift of myself. Saint Thérèse, pray for us.

Lesson Eighty-Five — Bearing Another's Defects

Lesson: Sister Thérèse received many graces during her final years. Among them was the grace to understand the command of Jesus to love as He loved. She noted that this was not just an invitation, it was a "command." And Jesus would not command something that could not be accomplished. Thus, she arrived at two conclusions regarding this precept of love.

First, she understood that "charity consists in bearing all our neighbours' defects—not being surprised at their weakness, but edified at their smallest virtues." This was no small task. It was so very easy to see the many faults of her sisters. It was not so easy to look deeper to see all of their virtues. However, Sister Thérèse rejoiced in this discovery and made it her mission to seek out virtue, no matter how small or hidden.

> If I wish to increase this love in my heart, and the devil tries to bring before me the defects of a Sister, I hasten to look for her virtues, her good motives; I call to mind that though I may have seen her fall once, no doubt she has gained many victories over herself, which in her humility she conceals.

Second, Sister Thérèse was aware of the fact that she was not capable of loving her sisters as Jesus loved them; she needed Jesus to do it in her. "Unless within me Thou lovest them, dear Lord!" she exclaimed. This was a beautiful realization for Sister Thérèse, that she could not love her sisters unless it was Jesus loving them within her and through her.

> Yes, I know when I show charity to others, it is simply Jesus acting in me, and the more closely I am united to Him, the more dearly I love my Sisters.

The Lord would not command perfect love of neighbor unless He provided the way. And the way was for Him to love others through us. Sister Thérèse discovered this lesson and fully assented to its practice.

Reflection: Toward whom do you need to increase your charity? Whose faults do you dwell on? Perhaps a family member, neighbor or coworker manifests faults that you tend to criticize, either to others or within your own mind. If so, then seek to imitate the precept of love as Saint Thérèse did.

First, look deeper and discover the virtue in that person's soul. It is there, sometimes hidden, but there waiting to be discovered and loved by you.

Second, know that you are incapable of love on your own. It is an impossible task. Only if you allow Jesus to live in you and love through you will you be able to fulfill the precept of charity to which you are called.

Identify a few concrete situations and at least one person in your life with whom you need to grow in charity. Pray for those you identify and open your heart to God's grace so that He may come and love through you.

Dearest Saint Thérèse, you heard the call to perfect love and responded with your whole heart. You allowed the love of your Lord to live in you and to love your sisters through you. Pray for me, that I may seek to love others as Jesus loves them, relying only upon His love and His Heart living in me. Saint Thérèse, pray for us.

Lesson Eighty-Six — A Sweet Smile

Lesson: Sister Thérèse understood well that charity is not primarily something that is felt; rather, it is a virtue that is expressed in deeds. Thus, she set out on a mission of love. She especially sought to show love to those who were most difficult to love.

> A holy nun of our community annoyed me in all that she did; the devil must have had something to do with it, and he it was undoubtedly who made me see in her so many disagreeable points. I did not want to yield to my natural antipathy...

Sister Thérèse did not give in to her natural animosity but instead chose to pray for this sister every time she encountered her. Additionally, Sister Thérèse looked beyond the surface and offered praise to God for the virtues she discovered underneath, praising the Creator for His beautiful creation.

Sister Thérèse did not stop with prayer and interior love; she also treated this sister with great affection and expressed her love with such regularity that this disagreeable sister was left confused as to why Sister Thérèse was so kind to her.

> "My dear Soeur Thérèse, tell me what attraction you find in me, for whenever we meet, you greet me with such a sweet smile." Ah! What attracted me was Jesus hidden in the depths of her soul—Jesus who maketh sweet even that which is most bitter.

What a powerful lesson of love. To love another to such a degree that the other is captivated by your love is charitable.

To do so toward one whom you find naturally disagreeable is saintly. Sister Thérèse turned what many people would find divisive into something unifying and holy. Thus, her lesson on the precept of charity was well-lived.

Reflection: Is there someone in your life whom you dislike? Does that person know you dislike him or her? If so, then God has given you the perfect person to love with much kindness. Even if you have hidden your dislike well, seek to love that person with much kindness and affection.

Who is that person? Or, perhaps several people come to mind. Choosing to love those who are difficult to love is not only a blessing to them, it is also a blessing to you. Seek to bring God's blessings into your own life and into the lives of those who are difficult, and you will see difficulties transformed by love.

Dearest Saint Thérèse, you charitably sought out the sister who was most difficult to love and loved her with your thoughts, words and actions. Your love was pure love, because it was not motivated by delight but by choice. Pray for me, that I may choose to love all people in every circumstance of my life. May I never shy away from love and allow love to transform even the most difficult relationship in my life. Saint Thérèse, pray for us.

Lesson Eighty-Seven — Fleeing Certain Defeat

Lesson: At times, we find ourselves in what could be termed a "lose-lose" battle. During her novitiate, Sister Thérèse found herself in such situations. For example, on one occasion she was unjustly accused of something quite trivial. Though it was minor, she immediately had a burning desire to defend herself. However, she realized that if she gave in to her impulse to defend herself, she would be giving in to pride and lose her peace of mind. On the other hand, she perceived that she was too weak to endure the false criticism. So what was she to do?

> ...my last chance of safety lay in flight. No sooner thought than done. I hurried away, but my heart beat so violently, I could not go far, and I was obliged to sit down on the stairs to enjoy in quiet the fruit of my victory. This is an odd kind of courage, undoubtedly, but I think it is best not to expose oneself in the face of certain defeat.

Sister Thérèse manifested a beautiful act of humility by admitting, first to herself, that she was not strong enough in virtue at the time to endure false judgment. She chose to flee "certain defeat." By fleeing the situation, she settled on the best path open to her at that moment. Of course, as the years went by Sister Thérèse grew in enough virtue to endure even the harshest criticism. But at the time, she knew herself and made the prudent choice to flee from this occasion of sin.

Reflection: Each one of us will face occasions of sin in our lives. At times, we may be tempted by others to join in gossip or criticism of another. Or, we might be the object of criticism and will be tempted to anger. At other times, another sin might tempt us, and we might find ourselves too weak to resist.

Remember the example of Sister Thérèse in those moments. Flee, run, hide and humbly admit you are too weak to endure the temptation. Fleeing may not be the most virtuous act of courage in the face of sin, but it might be the safest.

Reflect especially upon any regular situation you encounter in which this method might be your best option. Do not be ashamed to admit your weakness and your past failures. And do not be too proud to admit that this is your best option at times. Seek to imitate the humility of Sister Thérèse, and you will be on the path to greater virtue.

Saint Thérèse, you were aware of your weakness and your need to flee from an occasion of sin rather than to be drawn into a situation of certain defeat. Pray for me, that I may have the wisdom necessary to flee from occasions of sin when I know I lack the virtue to stay and fight. May this prudence guide me as it did you, so that I can continue down the path of virtue to which I am called. Saint Thérèse, pray for us.

Lesson Eighty-Eight — A Double Embrace of Poverty

Lesson: Sister Thérèse and her Carmelite sisters took a vow of poverty. With this vow they renounced all personal possessions and considered all that they used as belonging not to them but to God and the community. For example, when referring to her cell, she called it "our" cell. Her lamp was "our" lamp, and everything else she used was not hers but was shared by the community. This act of poverty helped each sister grow in detachment to all things of this world.

However, Sister Thérèse slowly came to discover a new form of attachment within the community which demanded a new form of poverty. This new poverty was in regard to "gifts of the intellect" and every good idea spoken of among the sisters.

Sister Thérèse had many deep insights, and she shared them freely among her sisters. At times, she noticed that a sister would repeat the "word of wisdom" without attributing it to Sister Thérèse. In pondering this, she realized that this was a new form of poverty, an intellectual and spiritual poverty to which she was called. Her ideas were not hers at all, they were God's, and because they were God's, they were given to all the sisters to use as their own.

> If it happens that a thought of mine should please my Sisters, I find it quite easy to let them regard it as their own. My thoughts belong to the Holy Ghost. They are not mine.

This new poverty of Sister Thérèse was also an act of great humility. Humility is this: we know the truth about ourselves, and the "truth" is that all wisdom and goodness are from God. Understanding this allowed this saintly sister to consider all of her thoughts as "our" thoughts.

Reflection: Though most of us are not called to a vow of poverty, we are called to the same spiritual and intellectual poverty to which Sister Thérèse refers. She discovered that God would inspire her at times with much wisdom. When she shared that wisdom, it was tempting to want others to acknowledge where it came from. But where did it come from? It came from the Holy Spirit.

Reflect upon those ideas, activities or acts of charity to which you have devoted much time and energy. Do you seek to possess these as your own or are you able to point to God as their origin and source?

Seek to give God all the credit for the good in your life and give to Him all the glory. This form of spiritual poverty will not be the cause of loss in your life; it will be the cause of much gain as you share freely all that God has given to you.

Saint Thérèse, you came to understand that all you had, including every good idea, came from God, belonged to God and was to be used by whomever God so willed. Pray for me, that I may also discover this form of spiritual poverty in life and may never seek to act in a selfish or greedy way. May I see God as the source of all good things and give glory only to Him. Saint Thérèse, pray for us.

Lesson Eighty-Nine — The Little Brush

Lesson: Sister Thérèse was aware of the work of God, the Master Artist, Who was creating various masterpieces in the souls of the sisters. God would use the Mother Superior and Novice Mistress as the "big brush" to form and shape the sisters, but at times Sister Thérèse was used to "fill in the minor details" as a "little brush" of God's grace and direction.

It was on December 8, 1892 that God used Sister Thérèse for the first time as a "little brush" for one such sister.

Sister Thérèse had kindled a holy friendship with a sister, and they enjoyed many spiritual discussions that helped them both grow in their love of God. However, eventually Sister Thérèse began to realize that their conversations were becoming increasingly secular and worldly. As a result, she prayed that God would help her to share this concern with her friend. She did so, and the other sister received the correction with much love, asking Sister Thérèse to bring to her any similar corrections she had in the future. Their friendship was deepened and became like a "strong city."

Later, when Sister Thérèse was given the responsibility of guiding the novices, she perceived many ways that God used her as this little brush to fill in the minor details of virtue within the souls of her sisters. God did all the work; Sister Thérèse was simply a small instrument of the Master Artist.

> From afar it seems so easy to do good to souls, to teach them to love God more, and to model them according to one's own ideas. But, when we draw nearer, we quickly feel that without God's help this is quite as impossible as to bring back the sun when once it has set. We must forget ourselves, and put aside our tastes and ideas, and guide souls not by our own way, but along the path which Our Lord points out.

Reflection: God wants to use you in countless "little" ways to help others grow in virtue and holiness. Sometimes we have "visions of grandeur" and come up with ways in which we will do great things for God. But God does not need a new "Master Artist." He and He alone fulfills this role. What He needs is "little brushes" through whom He can help be attentive to the smallest details of life.

Reflect upon your mission to imitate Sister Thérèse in being a little brush. Seek to be open to the many ways that God might want to use you. Doing so takes humility, since many of the tasks God gives us are small and hidden. Are you willing to be used for such tasks?

Reflect upon being this "little brush" in imitation of Sister Thérèse and, as you do, rejoice that you are so privileged to be able to be used for such small things.

Dearest Saint Thérèse, you embraced the humble yet important role of being a little brush in the hand of God. As you did, God used you to help your sisters grow in virtue, even in the smallest of ways. Pray for me, that I may also offer myself to God, the Master Artist, so that He may use me as He wills. May I be a willing instrument of His love, mercy, correction and grace as He so deigns. Saint Thérèse, Pray for us.

Lesson Ninety — Waging War

Lesson: Being used as God's "little brush" to help paint the beautiful virtues of Heaven on the souls of her "little flock" of novices entrusted to her care was indeed a great privilege of Sister Thérèse. She embraced this responsibility with fervor, and there was little chance she would ever be accused of being "the hireling . . . who seeth the wolf coming and leaveth the sheep, and flieth" (John 10:12). She was diligent in her care and noted, "...what costs me more than all is having to observe their faults, their slightest imperfections, and wage war against them." But waging war on their imperfections out of love is exactly what she did.

> I know, dear Mother, that your little lambs find me severe; if they were to read these lines, they would say that, so far as they can see, it does not distress me to run after them, and show them how they have soiled their beautiful white fleece, or torn it in the brambles. Well, the little lambs may say what they like—in their hearts they know I love them dearly...

As with any family, a parent discovers that what works with one child doesn't always work with the other. Sister Thérèse discovered this same truth as she waged her war of love, allowing God to use her to form her little lambs.

> With some I must humble myself, and not shrink from acknowledging my own struggles and defeats; then they confess more readily the faults into which they fall, and are pleased that I know by experience what they suffer. With others, my only means of success is to be firm, and never go back on what I have once said; self-abasement would be taken for weakness.

Sister Thérèse loved with such depth that the Great Master Artist could use her in the most varied of ways. This "little brush" of God's mercy was truly a dedicated brush, accomplishing the most beautiful works of love by waging war on every spiritual imperfection that kept these little ones from divine union.

Reflection: When we love God above all things, this love cannot be contained. We cannot keep God to ourselves. Sister Thérèse discovered this lesson of love and fully dedicated herself to her little lambs, drawing out their smallest virtues and seeking to eliminate their slightest defect.

Do you love God with such depth that His love overflows from your heart to the hearts of others? Whom has God entrusted to you to care for, guide and form in His ways? Are you willing to let God use you in the way that others need, setting aside your own will, your own preferences and your own ideas so that God's will can be accomplished?

Reflect upon your love of others, especially those closest to you and those within your own family. Surrender yourself more deeply to the task of love and allow yourself, like Sister Thérèse, to be used to help others grow into the perfect masterpieces God is creating them to be.

Dearest Saint Thérèse, God used you in many and varied ways. At times you were severe, and at times you humbled yourself before others. Pray for me, that I may be used by God in accord with His perfect plan of love. May I act as an instrument of His love so that the love in my heart will overflow into the lives of others. Saint Thérèse, pray for us.

Lesson Ninety-One — Sister St. Peter

Lesson: As a novice, Sister Thérèse recalled a blessed opportunity she was given to show an ongoing act of charity toward one of the elderly sisters.

Shortly before Sister St. Peter became quite bedridden, it was necessary every evening, at ten minutes to six, for someone to leave meditation and take her to the refectory. It cost me a good deal to offer my services, for I knew the difficulty, or I should say the impossibility, of pleasing the poor invalid. But I did not want to lose such a good opportunity, for I recalled Our Lord's words: "As long as you did it to one of these my least brethren, you did it to Me" (Matthew 25:40).

Most people would see this duty as a burden, but Sister Thérèse discovered the hidden act of love to which she was called by patiently and lovingly serving this "poor invalid." For her daily act of love, Sister Thérèse received criticism from Sister St. Peter. She responded with more than patience; she responded with supernatural charity, which eventually won the heart of this elderly sister. Her love of Sister St. Peter reached a new height when, upon fulfilling the necessary duties to assist her in her frailty, Sister Thérèse went even further.

But I soon noticed that she found it very difficult to cut her bread, so I did not leave her till I had performed this last service. She was much touched by this attention on my part, for she had not expressed any wish on the subject; it was by this unsought-for kindness that I gained her entire confidence, and chiefly because—as I learnt later— at the end of my humble task I bestowed upon her my sweetest smile.

During one such occasion, Sister Thérèse pondered a clear contrast of experiences. One day, from outside the convent walls, she heard music from a local dance and pondered the enjoyment that those in the town were currently enjoying. She imagined the women dressed beautifully and treated with charm and respect. But her meditation took her further.

> Then I looked on the poor invalid I was tending. Instead of sweet music I heard her complaints, instead of rich gilding I saw the brick walls of our bare cloister, scarcely visible in the dim light. The contrast was very moving. Our Lord so illuminated my soul with the rays of truth, before which the pleasures of the world are but as darkness, that for a thousand years of such worldly delights, I would not have bartered even the ten minutes spent in my act of charity.

Sister Thérèse had discovered the immense joy of selfless service and sacrifice. The value of this act of charity far outweighed anything the world could offer. What a blessing to see these two contrasting situations through the eyes of divine love.

Reflection: Each one of us will encounter situations that at first seem to be burdensome, unjust, and at times even impossible to deal with. But those "opportunities" are just that: opportunities. They provide us the invitation to look deeper and discover the hidden value of service in the face of ridicule, disorder, ingratitude and even persecution.

How well do you look beyond the veneer of such situations in your daily life? Do you tend to complain about this person or that, about this situation or another? Most often, the situations or persons we complain about are the very situations and persons in which we will discover the greatest joys of life. Love, service, kindness and generosity in the face of ridicule, severity, persecution and injustice is one of the greatest opportunities we are given each day to discover and live the hidden joys of life.

Reflect upon what you complain about the most. Try to look at that situation or person in a new way today. Seek to follow the example of Sister Thérèse and allow yourself to discover the blessed opportunity that has been placed before you.

Dearest Saint Thérèse, you saw the angry complaints, ridicule and lack of gratitude of Sister St. Peter as a blessed opportunity and invitation to love to the greatest degree. Pray for me, that I may never shy away from opportunities of charity, especially when such an act requires the embrace of injustice. May I choose love above all things and never waver in this decision. Saint Thérèse, pray for us.

Lesson Ninety-Two — Musical Fidgeting

Lesson: Perhaps you have endured some minor annoyance which, though minor, occupied much of your attention. Sister Thérèse recounts a story of one sister who, during prayer in chapel, would "fidget" constantly. She would move, clang her rosary continuously, and be distracting in numerous ways. Though tempted to express her displeasure with this sister, Sister Thérèse chose, instead, to turn the "fidgeting" into music for the Lord.

> I kept quiet, but the effort cost me so much that sometimes I was bathed in perspiration, and my meditation consisted merely in suffering with patience. After a time I tried to endure it in peace and joy, at least deep down in my soul, and I strove to take actual pleasure in the disagreeable little noise. Instead of trying not to hear it, which was impossible, I set myself to listen, as though it had been some delightful music, and my meditation—which was not the "prayer of quiet"—was passed in offering this music to Our Lord.

On another occasion, a sister with whom she did the laundry regularly splashed Sister Thérèse with dirty water. Again, though tempted to anger, she let go of her annoyance and rejoiced in this little gift from God.

Some may say that Sister Thérèse simply made the best of these minor difficulties, but she did more than that. She allowed a temptation to become a source of prayer and grace. Allowing annoyances to become music for the Lord was not just a coping mechanism Sister Thérèse used. Rather, it became a prayer because it was an offering, a sacrifice to God. Prayer is sacrifice, and every temptation we receive or every displeasure we endure is an opportunity for either frustration or grace, anger or mercy, annoyance or prayer.

Reflection: What comes to mind as a source of frustration in your daily life? Is there a habit of another, a rule at work, an injustice you daily face that tempts you to annoyance, frustration and even anger?

Ponder the "fidgeting" that you encounter on a regular basis and consider the action of Sister Thérèse as the solution. Do you know that every annoyance you encounter is a potential prayer of offering to God? Though this might not be hard to accept, it can be hard to put into practice.

As you reflect upon the opportunities in your life to imitate the virtue and prayer of Sister Thérèse, be concrete. Make a specific decision to offer some displeasure to God as a prayer of sacrifice. God will receive it, and you will receive much grace, enabling you to ultimately rejoice in the gift of "fidgeting" you have been given.

Dearest Saint Thérèse, you beautifully received the constant annoyance of this sister's fidgeting as a gift and offered that gift to God as a prayerful sacrifice, a musical hymn of praise. Pray for me, that I will never allow minor displeasures in life to deter me from a life of virtue. May all things truly work for good and become part of the complete surrender of my life to God. I desire that my whole life becomes a beautiful song of praise to Him Who is worthy of all praise. Saint Thérèse, pray for us.

Lesson Ninety-Three — Brother Priests

Lesson: Sister Thérèse had a deep love for priests and prayed for them often. She pondered how blessed she would have been if she had a brother who was a priest.

> For years I had cherished a longing which seemed impossible of realisation—to have a brother a Priest. I often used to think that if my little brothers had not gone to Heaven, I should have had the happiness of seeing them at the Altar. I greatly regretted being deprived of this joy. Yet God went beyond my dream; I only asked for one brother who would remember me each day at the Holy Altar, and He has united me in the bonds of spiritual friendship with two of His apostles.

Her first priestly brother was Father Maurice Bellière who contacted Carmel while he was still a seminarian, seeking a Carmelite sister to pray for him. The seminarian, L'abbé Bellière at the time, was a subdeacon and a member of the White Fathers. He had been orphaned at the age of three and raised by his aunt. He was twenty-one years old when he contacted Mother Agnes of Jesus, asking for a Carmelite sister.

The year Sister Thérèse adopted her first brother, the Carmelite sisters received a request from Father Adolphe Rouland of the Society of the Foreign Missions that he receive a spiritual sister. Once again, Sister Thérèse was assigned the task.

Two brother priests! What a blessing to her she thought. However, at that time, these two priests had no idea how blessed they were to have received the gift of such a spiritual sister.

Sister Thérèse prayed fervently for these two brothers but did more than that. Though she had great respect and admiration for the priestly office, she did not shy away from offering advice, correction, teaching and spiritual exhortations to her brothers. Her respect for them and for their mission led her to take her spiritual sisterhood seriously, doing all she could to assure their sanctity. Most notable was the joy in which she received her new brothers.

> Mother, I cannot tell you how happy this made me. Such unlooked-for fulfillment of my desire awoke in my heart the joy of a child; it carried me back to those early days, when pleasures were so keen, that my heart seemed too small to contain them. Years had passed since I had tasted a like happiness, so fresh, so unfamiliar, as if forgotten chords had been stirred within me.

Sister Thérèse was ecstatic at the thought of having a priest as an adopted brother. This did show her love for the priesthood, but it even more clearly showed her love for Christ and for the way that He comes to everyone through the priest.

Reflection: Though not all of us will be given a special relationship with a priest, we must all cherish those whom God does put in our lives. Whom has God given to you to love and care for in a particular way? For most people, these special friendships are those within their own family.

Do you see the people in your family as gifts from God for whom you must pray, encourage, support and exhort in holiness? Sister Thérèse was thrilled to have two priests as adopted brothers, but we must all be just as thrilled to have our parents, grandparents, children, siblings and other relatives as our true brothers and sisters in Christ. And if God has placed a desire within your heart to pray for priests and to adopt one as a "spiritual brother" in Christ, see this as a blessed invitation to support them in their sacred ministry. Though the Carmelite mission was especially focused on prayer for priests, we are all called to pray for them.

Reflect upon the joy in the heart of Sister Thérèse as she loved her priest brothers and work to foster that same joy in your heart toward your family. They were given to you as a gift from God. You must love them, care for them and do all you can to help them fulfill their mission on Earth and attain the joys of Heaven.

Dearest Saint Thérèse, you counted it as pure joy to receive these two priests as your spiritual brothers. You prayed for them, supported them and taught them your "Little Way." Pray for me, that I may be filled with joy over those God has put into my life. May I do all I can to love them and care for them so as to help them on their way toward the fulfillment of their holy mission. Saint Thérèse, pray for us.

Lesson Ninety-Four — "Draw me—we will run!"

Lesson: Sister Thérèse spent much of her later years in the convent giving herself in love to her "little lambs" and to the two priests whom God entrusted to her sisterly care. In addition to them, she felt a strong draw to love and pray for all missionaries and for the entire Church.

One day after Holy Communion, Sister Thérèse reflected upon the Canticle "Draw me: we will run after Thee to the odour of Thy ointments" (Canticle 1:3). In pondering this Canticle, she was especially drawn to the prayer "Draw me." As she pondered this prayer in light of the love she had for those whom God had entrusted to her care (her sisters, her brother priests, all missionaries and the whole Church), she was aware of the fact that she could not possibly know every one of their needs to sufficiently present each need to God. However, Sister Thérèse did discover that if she loved them with the deepest love, then their souls also would be drawn to God as she ran toward Him.

> O my Jesus, there is no need to say: "In drawing me, draw also the souls that I love": these words, "Draw me," suffice. When a soul has let herself be taken captive by the inebriating odour of Thy perfumes, she cannot run alone; as a natural consequence of her attraction towards Thee, the souls of all those she loves are drawn in her train.

Thus, Sister Thérèse discovered that the best way to pray for souls was to love them, carry them in her heart, and then allow her heart to be drawn to God. In doing so, she understood that this was the best way to pray for souls. She further reflected upon the great prayer of Jesus Himself from the Gospel of John.

> I pray for them: I pray not for the world, but for them whom Thou hast given me, because they are Thine. And all mine are Thine, and Thine are mine; and I am glorified in them. And now I am no more

in the world, and these are in the world, and I come to Thee. Holy Father, keep them in Thy name, whom Thou hast given me, that they may be one, as we also are one (cf. John 17).

Jesus loved those whom the Father entrusted to Him, and He prayed for them by coming to the Father with them in His Heart. As Jesus was one with the Father, so also His union with the Father brought forth the union of those He held in His Heart with the Father. Sister Thérèse discovered that she, too, must carry those whom God had entrusted to her in her heart and she was to offer her heart to God. In doing so, she offered those she loved to God. The offering of her heart and the offering of those in her heart were one and the same act of offering.

Reflection: God entrusts to each of us specific people whom we must love with profound love. He has entrusted specific people to us more than others. We will never offer them a greater act than to love them dearly, hold them in our heart, and offer that heart to God.

Whom has God given to you to love in a special way? Spouses especially are called to this love, as are parents. From time to time, God also might entrust other souls to your love. You might not be able to solve all their problems, understand every one of their needs or be there for them every time they fall. But you are able to love them so deeply that you carry them in your heart.

Reflect upon those you do carry in your heart. As you call them to mind, reflect also upon the words "Draw me." Hear God call to you, drawing you to Himself. Know that, as you go to Him and surrender your heart to Him, you are entrusting those special souls in your life to God. This form of prayer is the best prayer of intercession you can offer.

Dearest Saint Thérèse, you loved those whom God had entrusted to you with a deep and burning love. You carried them in your heart and offered that holy heart to God, also entrusting those whom you loved to God. Pray for me, that I may also love those whom God has entrusted to me with the deepest love. As I carry them in my heart, may I offer my heart to God as He draws me, so that my heart and those whom I love will be united to God in pure love. Saint Thérèse, pray for us.

Chapter Ten

Love in the Heart of the Church

Letter to Sister Marie of the Sacred Heart — Manuscript B

September 1896

Lesson Ninety-Five — Possessed

Lesson: On September 13, 1896, Sister Marie of the Sacred Heart (Thérèse's sister), wrote to Sister Thérèse asking her for a short note that expressed the secrets of her heart—the secrets God had confided to her. "The secrets of Jesus to Thérèse are sweet, and I would like to hear about them once again." That night, Sister Thérèse wrote a beautiful note to Sister Marie and included a reflection she had written five days earlier, September 8, the day after Sister Thérèse had begun a ten-day retreat. This letter and her enclosed reflection make up the last chapter of the *Story of a Soul.* Upon reading these pages, Sister Marie wrote back to Sister Thérèse expressing her gratitude and awe.

> Oh! I wanted to cry when I read these lines that are not from earth but an echo from the Heart of God...Do you want me to tell you? Well, you are possessed by God, but what is called...absolutely possessed, just as the wicked are possessed by the devil.

Sister Marie went on to say, "I would like to be possessed, too, by good Jesus. However, I love you so much that I rejoice when seeing you are more privileged than I am." Upon reading these words, Sister Thérèse wrote back to her sister.

> ...I am sure that God would not give you the desire to be POSSESSED by *Him*, by His *Merciful Love* if He were not reserving this favor for you...or rather He has already given it to you, since you have given yourself to *Him*, since you *desire* to be consumed by *Him*, and since God never gives desires that He cannot realize...

The love shared by these two sisters was quite profound. They each deeply desired that the other know Jesus and allow herself to be deeply loved by Him, consumed by Him and possessed by Him. Each sister desired it more for the other than for herself. They admired each other, encouraged each other, shared their hearts with each other and were deeply united with each other. Their love for each other was only possible as a result of their shared love for and union with Jesus. Recall that the first eight chapters of *Story of a Soul* were written at the request of Sister Marie who asked Mother Agnes of Jesus to order Sister Thérèse to write her childhood memories so they could enjoy them. Chapter 10's reflections are the fruit of the love of these two sisters.

Reflection: When you think of those whom you love, what is your desire for them? Is it riches, worldly success, popularity, or is it that they become consumed and even possessed by God? The greatest love we can have for others is that they are perfectly united to God.

Ponder the affectionate words shared between these sisters, and then ponder the relationships in your life. The love they shared is a perfect example of the love we must all strive to obtain for each other.

Dearest Saint Thérèse, your love for your sister Marie was a love that desired her perfect union with God. She, in turn, desired your perfect union with God and was grateful for the beauty of your soul. Pray for me, that I may seek this love in every relationship I have. May I desire this greatest good for everyone I know and do all I can to help all those in my life on their ways toward holiness. Saint Thérèse, pray for us.

Lesson Ninety-Six — Sweet Odor of the Beloved

Lesson: Sister Thérèse thirsted for Jesus with a burning thirst. She longed to love her Lord with every fiber of her being. To her, everything about Him was like a sweet fragrance, drawing her closer to her Beloved.

> Dear Mother, I have still to tell you what I understand by the *sweet odour of the Beloved*. As Our Lord is now in Heaven, I can only follow Him by the footprints He has left—footprints full of life, full of fragrance. I have only to open the Holy Gospels and at once I breathe the perfume of Jesus, and then I know which way to run...

She pondered the many stories in Scripture that taught her how to come to Jesus. She reflected upon the Publican who hid his face and cried for mercy. She reflected upon the Apostles who answered the call with haste. She reflected upon Mary who sat at the feet of Jesus, adoring Him with love. And she reflected upon the great sinners, such as the woman caught in adultery and the woman at the well. In all of these figures and in the many other passages of the Scriptures, Sister Thérèse learned how to run to Jesus and love Him as her Beloved. These Scriptures provided her with the scent of her Beloved, and she breathed in that scent deeply.

She also discovered something that drew her ever closer to her divine King. She discovered that He thirsted for her! For example, when she thought about the woman at the well, she understood that when Jesus asked her for a drink, He was speaking about a thirst He had for her soul.

These reflections led her to deepen her resolve to live out the Little Way that she had embraced as her quickest and easiest way to Heaven. How could her Beloved refuse her if He desired her so deeply? If she simply ran to Him, pursued Him and sought to quench His thirst for her, He could not resist her.

> Dearest Mother, if weak and imperfect souls like mine felt what I feel, none would despair of reaching the summit of the Mountain of Love, since Jesus does not ask for great deeds, but only for gratitude and self-surrender.

Sister Thérèse was filled with gratitude and love for her Savior. It was this unshakeable confidence that enabled her to know with certitude that even if she committed all the sins in the world, those sins "would disappear in an instant, even as a drop of water cast into a flaming furnace." She knew that if she, or any sinner on Earth, ran to the arms of the Savior, He would not resist His beloved's love.

Reflection: How much confidence do you have in God's mercy? Our confidence should never be in our own goodness or merit. Sister Thérèse understood this well. Our confidence must be in God and God alone. His mercy is so great that nothing can keep us from Him if we allow Him to draw us to Himself.

Reflect upon your own life and especially your sin. As you do, consider that sin to be like a single drop of water falling into the most ferocious and blazing furnace of God's love.

Whatever it is that you feel keeps you from Jesus, let it be consumed by His infinite mercy. God's love can consume the most grievous sin.

Seek to understand and live this Little Way of Saint Thérèse and you will find yourself delighting in the sweet fragrance of His mercy, leading you to a deeper communion of love than you could imagine.

Dearest Saint Thérèse, your love for your Beloved is only outdone by His love for you. Pray for me, that I may grow in confidence in the mercy of God and that I may allow His mercy to transform my soul, so that I can love Him with all that I am. May nothing keep me from His love—no sin, no weakness, no fault. May I learn to live the Little Way of love that you discovered, so that I may be one with Him Who loves me so dearly. Saint Thérèse, pray for us.

Lesson Ninety-Seven — Venerable Mother Anne of Jesus

Lesson: During the final years of Sister Thérèse's life, she endured a deep darkness in which she loved Jesus with the deepest love but could not sense the reality of Heaven. This darkness was a gift given by God to draw her ever closer to Him through profound acts of faith, hope and love.

In the midst of this darkness, God gave her a special consolation one night that helped pierce the dark night she was experiencing. She had a dream about the foundress of her Carmelite community in Lisieux, Venerable Mother

Anne of Jesus. Up until this time, she had little devotion to Mother Anne and knew very little about her. But in her inspired dream, Mother Anne came to Sister Thérèse and reassured her twice that God was pleased with her. The countenance on Mother Anne's face was radiant, and her motherly assurance to Sister Thérèse was transforming. She reassured her that "The Good God asks no more of you, He is pleased, quite pleased." Then Sister Thérèse awoke.

> On waking, I realised that Heaven does indeed exist, and that this Heaven is peopled with souls who cherish me as their child, and this impression still remains with me—all the sweeter, because, up to that time, I had but little devotion to the Venerable Mother Anne of Jesus. I had never sought her help, and but rarely heard her name. And now I know and understand how constantly I was in her thoughts, and the knowledge adds to my love for her and for all the dear ones in my Father's Home.

This dream helped Sister Thérèse to penetrate the dark veil that hid from her the reality of Heaven. Heaven was real! And in Heaven, there are countless souls, such as Mother Anne of Jesus, who loved her and looked forward to her joining them soon in their Father's House.

Reflection: At times, God hides the mysteries of Heaven from us for our own good, to strengthen us in our faith and love of Him. Do you feel as though God is distant at times? If so, do not be discouraged. Instead, seek to deepen your love and make constant acts of faith in Him.

As you do so, know that He is purifying you and helping you to grow in virtue.

When God does give some consolation to you or some insight into His mercy, remember it, cherish it and cling to it. Sister Thérèse savored this dream for the rest of her life, especially when she suffered. Her remembrance of this encounter deepened her trust in God and her hope in Heaven. Today, that hope is fully realized for her and the veil of darkness will never cloud her vision again.

Dearest Saint Thérèse, you were given this deeply consoling dream as a lesson about Heaven. You clung to this lesson, pondered its meaning and allowed your memory of it to be a source of inspiration for the rest of your earthly life. Pray for me, that in times of darkness and confusion I will remember the sweet consolations God has given me, so that I will persevere through all things so as to one day enjoy the full vision of Heaven forever. Saint Thérèse, pray for us.

Lesson Ninety-Eight — "My Vocation is Love!"

Lesson: Sister Thérèse discovered within herself an infinite longing to love God in countless ways. She loved her vocation as a Carmelite nun but also saw great beauty in every vocation within the Church. In her longing, she couldn't shake the desire to embrace every vocation of every time.

> To be Thy Spouse, O my Jesus, to be a daughter of Carmel, and by my union with Thee to be the

mother of souls, should not all this content me? And yet other vocations make themselves felt—I feel called to the Priesthood and to the Apostolate—I would be a Martyr, a Doctor of the Church. I should like to accomplish the most heroic deeds—the spirit of the Crusader burns within me, and I long to die on the field of battle in defense of Holy Church.

She went on to ponder the great martyrs such as St. Bartholomew who was flayed alive for love of God, Saint John who was plunged into boiling oil, St. Ignatius of Antioch who was ground by the teeth of wild beasts, and St. Agnes and St. Cecilia who offered their necks to the sword of the executioner. She also pondered her heroine of France, Saint Joan of Arc, who fought for the faith on the battlefield. And to be a priest! To offer the Holy Mass! She was overwhelmed with love of every vocation and desired them all. How could she fulfill these deep longings to love God in so many ways? Her answer was discovered as she read Saint Paul as he spoke about the Body of Christ, the Church.

I knew that the Church has a heart, that this heart burns with love, and that it is love alone which gives life to its members. I knew that if this love were extinguished, the Apostles would no longer preach the Gospel, and the Martyrs would refuse to shed their blood. I understood that love embraces all vocations, that it is all things, and that it reaches out through all the ages, and to the uttermost limits of the earth, because it is eternal.

Then, beside myself with joy, I cried out: "O Jesus, my Love, at last I have found my vocation. My vocation is love! Yes, I have found my place in the bosom of the Church, and this place, O my God, Thou hast Thyself given to me: in the heart of the Church, my Mother, I will be LOVE! . . . Thus I shall be all things: thus will my dream be realised. . . ."

Sister Thérèse discovered her sacred vocation. She was to be the heart of the Church. She was to be love. In being LOVE, by incarnating love, she would be a member of every person, embrace every vocation and live that which was the motivating force of every saint. Love was the answer, and love would be her vocation!

Reflection: God gives each one of us a unique calling. We cannot accomplish every role and fulfill every need in a material way, but we can live the one central role of every vocation. We can live a vocation of love, for love is everything! By living love and by bringing more love into our world, we provide the fuel and heart of every vocation.

What is your role in society and especially within the Church? Whatever your particular vocation may be, do you seek to live it with the greatest love possible? If so, you, like Saint Thérèse, will add to every vocation and will enliven the entire Church with the Heart of Christ.

Reflect upon the universal call of every Christian to be the Heart of Christ in the midst of the Church. How you live the love in the Heart of Christ may differ from others, but it will be the same Heart and the same love lived by every saint of old, every living saint today and every saint who is to come.

Dearest Saint Thérèse, you discovered your universal vocation to love. You understood well that you were called to be the Heart of Christ alive within the Church. By being His Heart, you were all things. Pray for me, that I may also discover this universal call to love. May I live love and be the Heart of Christ in the unique way I am called, and may I do so with great zeal and fervor all the days of my life. Saint Thérèse, pray for us.

Lesson Ninety-Nine — A Little Bird; A Victim of Divine Love

Lesson: Sister Thérèse had discovered her vocation. She was to be love in the heart of the Church and in being love, she was to be all things. But how was she to love? How could she attain this high calling? Sister Thérèse was keenly aware of her littleness and weakness, yet she was also aware of her desire to aspire to the greatest heights of love!

> How can a soul so imperfect as mine aspire to the plenitude of Love? What is the key of this mystery? O my only Friend, why dost Thou not reserve these infinite longings to lofty souls, to the eagles that soar in the heights? Alas! I am but a poor little unfledged bird. I am not an eagle, I have but the eagle's eyes and heart! Yet, notwithstanding my exceeding littleness, I dare to gaze upon the Divine Sun of Love, and I burn to dart upwards unto Him!

> I would fly, I would imitate the eagles; but all that I
> can do is to lift up my little wings——it is beyond my
> feeble power to soar.

Her prayer and her ponderings led her to realize that the key to the fulfillment of her calling of love was indeed to remain little, a little bird. She would fix her eyes on Heaven and gaze at the Divine Sun of Love. She would be a willing participant in love, but she also knew that she was incapable of this high calling by herself. Therefore, it was her hope that God's love would accept her as a "victim." She would "count on the aid of Angels and Saints" and would keep her eyes fixed upon Jesus, so that she would become His prey, "Love's prey." She longed to have her Divine Eagle "swoop down" and bear her away "to the Source of all Love." The Divine Eagle had already descended to Earth, He remains here in the Sacred Host, but He also re-ascends to Heaven. She would love Him and become His prey, His victim of love, and thus ascend with Him by His strength alone. This was her only chance of fulfilling such a glorious call to love. This was her prayer for all who sought to live such a lofty vocation of LOVE.

> I ENTREAT THEE TO LET THY DIVINE
> EYES REST UPON A VAST NUMBER OF
> LITTLE SOULS, I ENTREAT THEE TO
> CHOOSE, IN THIS WORLD, A LEGION OF
> LITTLE VICTIMS OF THY LOVE.

Reflection: The depth and beauty of Sister Thérèse's discovery was awe-inspiring. She understood victimhood in a new way and understood that it was only in being a martyr for love, a victim of love, that she could attain the calling she received.

Ponder these deep insights from this little saint of God. Reflect upon her joy and enthusiasm at the discovery of her profound calling. Realize that God is calling you to the heights of greatness, but that you cannot attain this on your own. You can only allow yourself to become love's victim. In doing so, our great God will seize you in His love and take you to the glory to which He has called you. He will especially do this through your consumption of the Most Holy Eucharist. Your duty is to say "Yes" and to gaze at Him in joyful anticipation of Him accepting your life as a sacrifice, a holocaust of love.

If this language is new to you, ponder it over and over. Pray to Saint Thérèse and ask her to teach you her Little Way of love. Seek to understand and surrender yourself to this quickest and easiest way toward the fulfillment of the vocation to which you have been called. Become a Victim of Divine Love, an offering pleasing to our Divine Lord.

Dearest Saint Thérèse, you offered yourself to Jesus with the utmost confidence in His mercy. You were little, weak and incapable of attaining the high calling of love to which you were called. Yet you knew that if you offered yourself as a martyr, a victim, God would receive you and take you to the glory of Heaven. Pray for me, that I may discover this Little Way of love. May I also become love's victim and, in this act, achieve the fulfillment of the vocation to which I am called. Saint Thérèse, pray for us.

Epilogue

Death, Canonization and Devotion to the Little Flower

The preceding 99 lessons are taken from the three manuscripts Sister Thérèse wrote that make up the body of the *Story of a Soul*. However, as will be explained in the following pages, Manuscript C was never finished and, as a result, her story presented in the three manuscripts is unfinished.

The goal of this Epilogue is to offer you the end of the story as has carefully been recorded in various other ways, especially by her sisters. Thus, we conclude the beautiful story of Saint Thérèse of the Child Jesus and the Holy Face by sharing the details of her final months on Earth.

Overview

On January 20, 1896, Sister Thérèse finished the first manuscript (Manuscript A) of three that would eventually make up the *Story of a Soul*. After presenting it to Mother Agnes of Jesus, she continued with her life as a religious sister as usual. On Holy Thursday, April 2, 1896, Sister Thérèse received the "first announcement" of her illness and death when she coughed blood into her handkerchief. This happened again on Good Friday, April 3, and was described by Sister Thérèse as a "distant murmur which announced the approach of the Bridegroom." The approach of the Bridegroom brought with it a new and very intense suffering when on April 5 (Easter Sunday), Sister Thérèse entered into a *dark night of faith* by which she was stripped of all interior consolation and all sensible experience of the reality of Heaven. Everything interiorly was like "a wall which rises to the very heavens and shuts out the starry sky." She would remain in this dark night for the next eighteen months until her death. But she understood well that this dark night was a gift by which she could love God more freely and deeply, not because she felt close to Him, but because He was worthy of all her love. Even though this darkness was more painful than she could describe, she never lost her interior peace and began to experience all suffering as sweet.

It was in September, 1896, that Sister Thérèse wrote the second manuscript (Manuscript B) of the *Story of a Soul* in the form of a letter to her sister, Sister Marie of the Sacred

Heart. That manuscript is covered in Chapter Ten of this book.

Between the months of April–November 1896, Sister Thérèse continued to cough and show signs of tuberculosis. In November, there was talk about her going to a mission Carmel in Hanoï, since the sisters there deeply desired her. Sister Thérèse began a novena to the Venerable Théophane Vénard, a martyr whose life she had recently become acquainted with, seeking a cure from her illness. However, instead of recovering, her condition worsened and she continued to slowly decline over the next year. Though she had some good weeks, Sister Thérèse would eventually go home to her Beloved Spouse as a "Martyr of Love" on September 30, 1897, surrounded by her sisters and all in her community. Her dying words were, "Oh!... I love Him!... My God, I...love...Thee!"

April–May 1897

Sister Thérèse had been suffering from the effects of tuberculosis for one full year when in April, 1897, her condition worsened again. On April 6, 1897, Sister Agnes began to write down her conversations with Sister Thérèse in a yellow notebook. Later, this notebook would be published under the title *Her Last Conversations*. Sister Agnes intuitively knew, by divine inspiration, that the words spoken by her sister in the coming months needed to be recorded. She followed that divine inspiration and, through these recorded words, Sister Agnes invites us all to walk with this little saint through her last agony.

As time went on, and as Sister Thérèse's condition continued to worsen, the sisters were aware that she might not live long. One sister was overheard saying of her, "Soeur Thérèse will not live long, and really sometimes I wonder what our Mother Prioress will find to say about her when she dies. She will be sorely puzzled, for this little Sister, amiable as she is, has certainly never done anything worth speaking about." Little did this sister realize that Sister Thérèse would one day be a Doctor of the Church and would be spoken of as one of the greatest saints ever to live.

June–July 1897

On June 3, at the petitioning of Sister Agnes, Mother Marie de Gonzague ordered Sister Thérèse to complete her autobiography. The first manuscript she wrote was finished in January of the previous year but only covered her childhood through her profession as a religious sister. Sister Agnes wanted more. So Sister Thérèse was ordered, despite her poor health, to write about her life as a religious sister (Manuscript C). Again, this was due to the loving spiritual intuition of her dear sister and second mother, Pauline, Sister Agnes of Jesus.

As mentioned, this manuscript is covered in Chapter Nine of this book. Though this section of her autobiography shares much about her Little Way, her love of God and her motherly care for her "little lambs," one thing is noticeably absent. Nowhere does this manuscript give the suggestion that Sister Thérèse was writing this manuscript while bedridden and gravely ill. It was as if her present illness had no effect upon her writing. Instead, she wrote for God and God alone, sharing all that God had done in her and through her, expressing especially her discovery of her *little way*.

On the evening of July 15, Sister Thérèse composed the following beautiful canticle of love to our Lord to be used as a prelude to receiving Holy Communion the next day on the great Feast of Our Lady of Mount Carmel:

> Thou know'st the baseness of my soul, O Lord, Yet fearest not to stoop and enter me. Come to my heart, O Sacrament adored! Come to my heart . . . it craveth but for Thee! And when Thou comest, straightway let me die Of very love for Thee; this boon impart! Oh, hearken Jesus, to my suppliant cry: Come to my heart!

By the end of July, her condition had worsened to the point that she received Extreme Unction (Last Rites) on July 30. The reception of this Sacrament filled her with great joy, since she knew it was a preparation for her final journey home.

> The door of my dark prison is ajar. I am steeped in joy, especially since our Father Superior has assured me that to-day my soul is like unto that of a little child after Baptism.

Though Sister Thérèse was ready to meet her Jesus, she would suffer for two more months. She prayed to our Lady, saying, "...I only beseech Our Lady to remind her Jesus of the title of *Thief*, which He takes to Himself in the Gospels, so that He may not forget to come and carry me away." How she longed to be fully immersed in the life of Heaven.

Between July 6 and August 5, she coughed blood twenty times. As a result, she was moved to the infirmary on July 8 where she remained until her death. In early July, Sister Thérèse gave up her pen, leaving her final manuscript unfinished. She was too ill to continue, so her story would have to be spoken by her suffering and by the words recorded by her sisters, especially by Sister Agnes. However, during the months of July and August she did find the strength to compose eighteen letters to family, her missionary priest brothers and to other Carmelites.

August 1897

August brought with it even more suffering. Over and over, Sister Thérèse was heard repeating, "Oh! how necessary it is to pray for the agonising! If one only knew!" As she suffered greatly, she never stopped trusting in the grace of God and never stopped uniting her sufferings to Jesus. One night, after suffering many interior afflictions from the evil one, she begged the sister who was caring for her to sprinkle her bed with Holy Water. The sister did that and also lit a holy candle and the attacks went away.

> I am besieged by the devil. I do not see him, but I feel him; he torments me and holds me with a grip of iron, that I may not find one crumb of comfort; he augments my woes, that I may be driven to despair. . . . And I cannot pray. I can only look at Our Blessed Lady and say: "Jesus!" How needful is that prayer we use at Compline: 'Procul recedant somnia et noctium phantasmata!' ("Free us from the phantoms of the night.") Something mysterious is happening within me. I am not suffering for myself, but for some other soul, and satan is angry.

Between the dates of August 5 and 15, her health somewhat improved, which allowed for various letters to be written. However, by August 25 her health worsened again and she would write no more. Most of her time was spent in silence and suffering.

September 1897

It had been almost a year since Sister Thérèse had read about the Venerable Théophane Vénard, Martyr, and had prayed a novena to him for healing. She continued to have great devotion to him and kept a picture of him in the infirmary. She had also deeply desired a relic of him but had not received it, so she accepted it as the will of God. That changed on September 6 when Mother Marie brought to her the relic she so desired. Sister Thérèse kissed it repeatedly and explained why she loved him so much.

Théophane Vénard is a *little* saint; his life was not marked by anything extraordinary. He had an ardent devotion to Our Immaculate Mother and a tender love of his own family. And I, too, love my family with a tender love; I fail to understand those Saints who do not share my feelings. As a parting gift I have copied for you some passages from his last letters home. His soul and mine have many points of resemblance, and his words do but re-echo my thoughts.

Here is a copy of what Sister Thérèse copied from the the last letters of Venerable Théophane Vénard, Martyr. These letters express the same sentiments in the heart of Sister Thérèse, which is why she was so devoted to him.

I can find nothing on earth that can make me truly happy; the desires of my heart are too vast, and nothing of what the world calls happiness can satisfy it. Time for me will soon be no more, my thoughts are fixed on Eternity. My heart is full of peace, like a tranquil lake or a cloudless sky. I do not regret this life on earth. I thirst for the waters of Life Eternal.

Yet a little while and my soul will have quitted this earth, will have finished her exile, will have ended her combat. I go to Heaven. I am about to enter the Abode of the Blessed—to see what the eye hath never seen, to hear what the ear hath never heard, to enjoy those things the heart of man hath not conceived . . . I have reached the hour so coveted by us all. It is indeed true that Our Lord chooses the little ones to confound the great ones of this earth. I do not rely upon my own strength but upon Him Who, on the Cross, vanquished the powers of hell.

I am a spring flower which the Divine Master culls for His pleasure. We are all flowers, planted on this earth, and God will gather us in His own good time—some sooner, some later . . . I, little flower of one day, am the first to be gathered! But we shall meet again in Paradise, where lasting joy will be our portion.

Sister Teresa of the Child Jesus, using the words of the angelic martyr—Théophane Vénard."

Saint Théophane Vénard was a French missionary serving in Indochina. He was arrested in Vietnam on November 30, 1860, and was found guilty of proselytism shortly afterward. He remained imprisoned until he was beheaded February 2, 1861, in Tonkin, Vietnam at age 31. While in prison, during the months of December and January, Théophane wrote many beautiful letters to family and others. It is these letters to which Sister Thérèse refers above. On his way to his execution, the executioner asked what Théophane would give him if he made his death quick. The saint responded, "The longer it lasts, the better it will be." In 1909 he was beatified by Pope Pius X and canonized on June 19, 1988, by Pope John Paul II.

Toward the end of September, Sister Thérèse's suffering increased greatly to the point that she could hardly move or speak. Yet, despite her great pain, one night the infirmarian entered her room and found her lying with her hands raised to Heaven. The sister quickly informed Sister Thérèse that she should be sleeping. To that, she responded, "I cannot, Sister, I am suffering too much, so I am praying. . . ." The sister then asked, "And what do you say to Jesus?" Sister Thérèse responded, "I say nothing—I only love Him!"

One of her final notes was to Mother Marie. She desired to express her soul to her earlier in the day but could not. Eventually she found the strength to write what was on her heart.

> O my God! how good Thou art to the little Victim of Thy Merciful Love! Now, even when Thou joinest these bodily pains to those of my soul, I cannot bring myself to say: "The anguish of death hath encompassed me" (Cf. Ps. 17[18]:5). I rather cry out in my gratitude: "I have gone down into the valley of the shadow of death, but I fear no evil, because Thou, O Lord, art with me" (Cf. Ps. 22[23]:4).

September 30, 1897

The following account of the final day of Sister Thérèse is taken in its entirety from the epilogue of the 1912 publication of the *Story of a Soul* under the title: *Soeur Thérèse of Lisieux* (London: Burns, Oates & Washbourne, 1912; 8th ed., 1922), edited by Rev. T.N. Taylor.

> At last dawned the eternal day. It was Thursday, September 30, 1897. In the morning, the sweet Victim, her eyes fixed on Our Lady's statue, spoke

thus of her last night on earth: "Oh! with what fervour I have prayed to her! . . . And yet it has been pure agony, without a ray of consolation. . . . Earth's air is failing me: when shall I breathe the air of Heaven?"

For weeks she had been unable to raise herself in bed, but, at half-past two in the afternoon, she sat up and exclaimed: "Dear Mother, the chalice is full to overflowing! I could never have believed that it was possible to suffer so intensely. . . . I can only explain it by my extreme desire to save souls. . . ." And a little while after: "Yes, all that I have written about my thirst for suffering is really true! I do not regret having surrendered myself to Love."

She repeated these last words several times. A little later she added: "Mother, prepare me to die well." The good Mother Prioress encouraged her with these words: "My child, you are quite ready to appear before God, for you have always understood the virtue of humility." Then, in striking words, Thérèse bore witness to herself:

"Yes, I feel it; my soul has ever sought the truth. . . . I have understood humility of heart!"

. . . .

At half-past four, her agony began—the agony of this "Victim of Divine Love." When the Community gathered round her, she thanked them with the sweetest smile, and then, completely given over to love and suffering, the Crucifix clasped in her failing hands, she entered on the final combat. The sweat of death lay heavy on her brow . . . she trembled . . . but, as a pilot, when close to harbour, is not dismayed by the fury of the storm, so this soul, strong in faith, saw close at hand the beacon-lights of Heaven, and valiantly put forth every effort to reach the shore.

As the convent bells rang the evening Angelus, she fixed an inexpressible look upon the statue of the Immaculate Virgin, the Star of the Sea. Was it not the moment to repeat her beautiful prayer:

"O thou who camest to smile on me in the morn of my life, come once again and smile, Mother, for now it is eventide!" [From the last poem of Sister Thérèse.]

A few minutes after seven, turning to the Prioress, the poor little Martyr asked: "Mother, is it not the agony? . . . am I not going to die?" "Yes, my child, it is the agony, but Jesus perhaps wills that it be prolonged for some hours." In a sweet and plaintive voice she replied: "Ah, very well then . . . very well . . . I do not wish to suffer less!"

Then, looking at her crucifix:

"Oh! . . . I love Him! . . . My God, I . . . love . . . Thee!"

These were her last words. She had scarcely uttered them when, to our great surprise, she sank down quite suddenly, her head inclined a little to the right, in the attitude of the Virgin Martyrs offering themselves to the sword; or rather, as a Victim of Love, awaiting from the Divine Archer the fiery shaft, by which she longs to die.

Suddenly she raised herself, as though called by a mysterious voice; and opening her eyes, which shone with unutterable happiness and peace, fixed her gaze a little above the statue of Our Lady. Thus she remained for about the space of a *Credo,* when her blessed soul, now become the prey of the "Divine Eagle," was borne away to the heights of Heaven.

. . . .

A few days before her death, this little Saint had said: "The death of Love which I so much desire is that of Jesus upon the Cross." Her prayer was fully granted. Darkness enveloped her, and her soul was steeped in anguish. And yet, may we not apply to her also that sublime prophecy of St. John of the Cross, referring to souls consumed by the fire of Divine Love: "They die Victims of the onslaughts of Love, in raptured ecstasies—like the swan, whose song grows sweeter as death draws nigh. Wherefore the Psalmist declared: 'Precious in the sight of the Lord is the death of His Saints' (Ps. 115[116]:15). For then it is that the rivers of love burst forth from the soul and are whelmed in the Ocean of Divine Love."

No sooner had her spotless soul taken its flight than the joy of that last rapture imprinted itself on her brow, and a radiant smile illumined her face. We placed a palm-branch in her hand; and the lilies and roses that adorned her in death were figures of her white robe of baptism made red by her Martyrdom of Love.

On the Saturday and Sunday a large crowd passed before the grating of the nuns' chapel, to gaze on the mortal remains of the "Little Flower of Jesus." Hundreds of medals and rosaries were brought to touch the "Little Queen" as she lay in the triumphant beauty of her last sleep.

. . . .

On October 4, the day of the funeral, there gathered in the Chapel of the Carmel a goodly company of Priests. The honour was surely due to one who had prayed so earnestly for those called to that sacred office. After a last solemn blessing, this grain of priceless wheat was cast into the furrow by the hands of Holy Mother Church.

Who shall tell how many ripened ears have sprung forth since, how many the sheaves that are yet to come? "Amen, amen, I say to you, unless the grain of wheat, falling into the ground, die, itself remaineth alone. But if it die, it bringeth forth much fruit" (John 12:24, 25). Once more the word of the Divine Reaper has been magnificently fulfilled.

"I will spend my Heaven doing good on Earth"

Sister Thérèse had gone to her Beloved. Her dark night and suffering were over. But as for her mission, it had only begun. Even before her death, Sister Thérèse believed that she would spend her Heaven doing good on Earth. She revealed this mission to Sister Agnes one evening after receiving clarity in her heart about what God was about to do.

> Mother! some notes from a concert far away have just reached my ears, and have made me think that soon I shall be listening to the wondrous melodies of Paradise. The thought, however, gave me but a moment's joy—one hope alone makes my heart beat fast: the Love that I shall receive and the Love I shall be able to give!

> I feel that my mission is soon to begin—my mission to make others love God as I love Him . . . to each souls my *little way* . . .

In one of her letters to China she wrote:

> I trust fully that I shall not remain idle in Heaven; my desire is to continue my work for the Church and for souls. I ask this of God, and I am convinced He will hear my prayer. You see that if I quit the battle-field so soon, it is not from a selfish desire of repose. For a long time now, suffering has been my Heaven here upon earth, and I can hardly conceive how I shall become acclimatised to a land where joy

is unmixed with sorrow. Jesus will certainly have to work a complete change in my soul—else I could never support the ecstasies of Paradise.

Saint Thérèse did not remain idle in Heaven. God used her very quickly to spread her *little way* of love. On March 7, 1898, Bishop Hugonin, Bishop of Bayeux, gave permission for the first printing of the *Story of a Soul*. Two thousand copies were printed and distributed over the next year. In October 1899, a second edition of 4,000 copies was printed and distributed. Saint Thérèse was quickly becoming read and loved throughout France and across Europe.

Over the next several decades, devotion to Saint Thérèse grew rapidly. In January 1909, a Postulator and Vice-Postulator for the cause of canonization were named in Rome to begin studying her heroic virtues and sanctity. As her diary reached far and wide, letters were being sent to the Carmel in Lisieux in miraculous force. In 1914 about 200 letters were being received every day from the faithful who read her story and were inspired by her *little way*. In 1918, the Lisieux Carmel was receiving over 500 letters a day. And by 1923, the good sisters of Lisieux were receiving up to 1,000 letters every day singing the praises of Saint Thérèse.

In 1914, just seventeen years after her death, Pope Pius X signed a decree introducing her cause for beatification. It has been reported that he privately said at that time, "Sister Thérèse is the greatest saint of modern times." She was proclaimed a Venerable Servant of God on August 14, 1921, and beatified by Pope Pius XI on April 29, 1923.

It was the great day of May 17, 1925, that Blessed Thérèse was canonized by Pope Pius XI, becoming Saint Thérèse of the Child Jesus and the Holy Face. Present at her canonization was an audience of 60,000 people in St. Peter's Basilica. Approximately 500,000 came that evening to pray and celebrate in St. Peter's Square.

On October 19, 1997, she was declared a Doctor of the Church by Saint John Paul II.

Her spiritual legacy continued on July 2, 2015, when her sister Léonie was named the Venerable Léonie Martin and the cause of her beatification began. That same year, on October 18, 2015, Saint Thérèse's parents were canonized together, making them the first husband and wife to be canonized and the first canonized parents of an already canonized saint.

May the Little Way of Saint Thérèse be understood, loved and lived by many. She is indeed one of the greatest saints of our time, and she will continue her mission of spending her Heaven doing good on Earth.

Saint Thérèse, pray for us!

For more daily reflections books from *My Catholic Life!* visit our websites at:

www.mycatholic.life

www.catholic-daily-reflections.com

www.divinemercy.life

Made in the USA
Las Vegas, NV
19 August 2021

28445714R00142